T0418970

People in conflict tell stories about what they experienced – sometimes to mend the fabric of a newly-torn reality, or explore the meaning of what happened, or demonize their opponents, or justify their own behavior -- but *always* to discover a way out, or return to their own un-conflicted selves, or tell the story in a way that imparts insight into the deeper reasons why it happened, allowing it to be forgotten. Samantha Hardy, a self-confessed "pracademic," brings a wonderful combination of practical coaching and mediation skills, a high level of emotional insight, and a profound understanding of the nature of narrative and melodrama to this excellent and immensely useful book. Every practitioner will learn something from it and walk away with a deeper understanding of the role of melodrama and tragedy in conflict stories, and a great many practical coaching and mediation skills to boot! It is an enjoyable read and well worth the price.

Kenneth Cloke, Mediator and author of *The Dance of Opposites: Explorations in Mediation, Dialogue and Conflict Resolution Systems Design, USA*

Samantha Hardy offers people in workplace conflicts a user-friendly guide to hearing the story they are telling themselves about their troubles. Too often, this "melodramatic narrative" has itself become part of the problem. I especially appreciate Hardy's depiction of people's illusion that conflicts can end with some "dream justice" and her sobering reflection that the most useful stance for a coach may be what she delightfully calls the "bumbling helper".

Arthur W. Frank, Ph.D., author of *Letting Stories Breathe: a Socio-narratology*

Sam is inviting you to look at conflict through a whole new set of eyes. The unique and entertaining lens that she is offering is genres of literature. She has uncovered and is taking you on a journey to discover healthy and unhealthy conflict story patterns. These insights provide you with the power to (re)-write your own, or help others (re)-write their, conflict narratives in a way that helps define new ways for moving forward and find peace with the past. A must for conflict specialists and people who want to critically reflect on their own approach to conflict.

Claudia Butler, Professional Conflict Navigator, Australia

In this book Dr Hardy shares her conflict management journey from 'inspiration' to 'solution' via considered academic investigation. Dr Hardy's use of the melodrama and tragedy genres provides a relatable vehicle for a broad media-savvy audience looking to expand their conflict management comfort zone. These genres provide a viewing lens through which the reader can assimilate established conflict management theory and subsequently understand the relevance and impact of Dr Hardy's "REAL" Conflict Coaching System for their everyday personal and professional lives. This perspective provides an additional and cogent toolkit for ADR providers that is congruent with (but different to) the approaches and perspectives of other pioneers of the field.

Anthony Dilley, MBBS FRACS RAN(Retd). Surgical Educator with the Royal Australasian College of Surgeons

Samantha Hardy draws together her deep understanding of conflict narratives and her practical expertise as a conflict coach, manager and resolver to gift us all with tools to construct helpful stories about our part in the conflicts of life. By "all of us" I mean anybody who is a friend, supportive relative, colleague, manager of people in conflict as well as people who are interested in formal conflict coaching. The ability to listen for the conflict story is a general life improvement tool. This book equips us to help ourselves and to help others through an empowering and self-determining process.

Dr. Olivia Rundle, Senior Lecturer in Law, University of Tasmania, Australia

Dr. Sam Hardy brings a unique research driven approach to working with conflict stories that is empowering and enabling for people to discover the range of choices available to learn and grow through conflicts. I love the focus on helping people become more aware of the conflict stories they are telling themselves and others. Sam's method to work towards more empowering choice filled alternatives is practical and inspiring.

The book contains great examples, rich stories, and many references to other interesting authors, but most importantly shares a unique genre-based story approach to helping people find ways forward when stuck in conflict. I highly recommend this book!

Andrew Rixon PhD, Director, Babel Fish Group

Dr Samantha Hardy is one of Australia's leading authorities on the theory, philosophy and practice of dispute resolution.

The central premise of the book, that of helping people to work with those in conflict by supporting them and explaining practical techniques to manage and resolve their conflict, is achieved superbly by telling the stories of real people who have been through the wringer of disputation. Learning and teaching how to handle conflict is so much more powerful when it is presented through the technique of storytelling. I think this is one of the books most endearing qualities and makes it a must purchase for the many dispute resolution practitioners around the world.

The book will help people working with others in conflict to fully support them by understanding which areas of the conflict story to focus their attention on and using practical techniques will help people who are themselves in a conflict scenario to rewrite and enact a version of their conflict story that helps them to more constructively manage, and often resolve, their situation.

I can see this text being on the bookshelf of those who work with people in conflict such as: mediators; conflict coaches; managers; lawyers; HR staff; and, others who are involved in any dimension of conflict. It will also attract anyone who wishes to better understand their own experience of conflict.

David Spencer, Solicitor and Senior Lecturer in Law,

Dr Samantha Hardy's new book offers a fascinating insight into the role that conflict stories play in the way people engage in and communicate the conflict in their lives.

Presented in two parts, **Part 1** first explores the nature of melodramatic conflict stories. Hardy identifies the challenge they represent for those experiencing these stories and also those professionals seeking to support others to navigate them. She provides us with a useful explanation of how our 'capacity to manage conflict improves when a melodramatic story is developed into a tragic one.' She presents this as a more constructive and realistic conflict story, more accessible to scrutiny and learning.

Part 2 explores thoroughly the role of coaching to support others to develop their conflict stories and offers us a proposed conflict coaching system. For those of us who work in the coaching space she offers some particularly valuable advice to let go our desire to be the hero if we are going to help our clients be the hero of their own future.

Illustrated with useful stories from her own experience, Hardy also provides very useful further reading at the end of each chapter.

A really useful, accessible, and practical text for those interested to explore their own stories and for professionals engaged in coaching practice to support others to unpack and engage more effectively with theirs.

Dr Rosemary Howell, Professorial Visiting Fellow, University of New South Wales

Through Samantha's use of engaging and relatable cases, readers are bound to gain insights about how conflict stories are formed and conveyed. She also details a unique methodology for shifting such stories to be able to become its "hero" rather than remain in the more counterproductive stances commonly taken. To facilitate that shift Samantha shares a host of practical techniques for re-scripting perceptions and experiences in order to constructively find our own way through interpersonal conflict, and to support clients who want to do so.

Cinnie Noble, author of *Conflict Management Coaching: The CINERGY Model*

In this highly readable and engaging account, Samantha Hardy, a leading figure in narrative conflict coaching, takes the reader on a journey from a world of simplified, bounded, and polarized conflict stories to one in which flawed and uncertain characters strive with one another in ironic and complex struggles to coexist in an uncertain future. Drawing on a genre theory of narrative conflict, Hardy presents what may be the field's most user-friendly model of narrative intervention, complete with real world examples drawn from her practice. We learn how to use narrative techniques to help parties to see themselves in new stories that better approximate the worlds they actually live in, where villains have mixed motives, victims have agency, and heroes are not always available to save the day. Hardy's book will be a welcome addition to the library of anyone with an interest in narrative, peace, and conflict.

Solon Simmons, Associate Professor of Peace and Conflict Resolution/ Sociologist, George Mason University and author of *Root Narrative Theory and Conflict Resolution: Power, Justice and Values.*

In this book, Samantha Hardy explores in depth the meaning of conflict narratives for the occurrence, manifestation and management of interpersonal conflict. In doing so, Sam takes a unique approach, analysing conflict narratives through the lens of two types of drama: melodrama and tragedy. Sam uncovers how melodramatic conflict stories reinforce victimhood, helplessness and passivity of people in conflict, while tragic conflict stories allow for choices, change, agency and empowerment. Sam also explores the role of a conflict coach to help people in conflict change their melodramatic conflict story into a tragic one. Numerous and rich real-life examples are provided to illustrate in detail the melodramatic conflict stories that people in conflict tend to tell, as well as to demonstrate how conflict coaches can help to rewrite these stories so that people become aware of their choices and feel empowered to make changes and improve their situation. The book is a wonderful asset for anyone who works with people in conflict, including mediators, coaches, HR staff, managers, etc. Since the book presents well researched and evidence based information in an entertaining manner, it is also incredibly useful for those who are new to conflict resolution and for those who are training others to become conflict resolution practitioners. While the book focuses on interpersonal conflict, conflict narratives also play a critical role in larger scale conflicts I believe that its message finds application beyond the interpersonal context.

Judith Rafferty, Director, Conflict Management and Resolution Program, James Cook University

In *Conflict Coaching Fundamentals: Working With Conflict Stories*, Samantha Hardy offers a step-by-step practical guide to conflict coaching that makes excellent use of examples from her coaching practice in a book that is well-crafted and eminently readable. Her approach is grounded in an abiding belief in the dignity of her clients and a conviction that they have the inborn capacity to be self-aware and that they are fully able to find creative and practical solutions to their dilemmas. Using the metaphors of the melodramatic and tragic stories, she explains how our view of a conflict situation can restrict our choices and actions or encourage and support us in developing effective and practical paths out of the conflict. This book is both engaging—in the she brings vividly to life, we hear the voices of her clients who confront the challenges and struggles of being stuck in the quagmire of conflict—and instructive—clearly and creditably setting out the benefits of conflict coaching.

Michael Lang, author of *The Guide to Reflective Practice in Conflict Resolution*

CONFLICT COACHING FUNDAMENTALS

We naturally create stories to help us make meaning of our world, but in conflict situations the kinds of stories we typically tell ourselves can actually make it harder for us to manage and resolve the conflict constructively. This book provides an accessible framework for understanding why people tell their conflict stories the way they do and how to help them move away from conflict stories that prevent them from understanding and responding to conflict in an effective way.

Presented using highly engaging and accessible cases, the book is designed to help people working with others in conflict to fully support them by understanding which areas of the conflict story to focus their attention on and using practical techniques to support people to rewrite their story into a more constructive one to better manage the situation. The book also provides practical strategies to help people who are themselves in a conflict scenario to rewrite and enact a version of their conflict story that helps them to more constructively manage, and often resolve, their situation. A conflict management coaching system is introduced that is designed to address the particular problems created by dysfunctional conflict stories.

This is a book specifically for those who work with people in conflict (mediators, conflict coaches, managers, lawyers, human resources staff, teachers) and also for anyone who wishes to better understand their own experience of conflict.

Samantha Hardy PhD has over 25 years' international experience practicing and teaching conflict management. She is the lead trainer at CCIAcademy.com and the founder of the REAL Conflict Coaching System™. She provides conflict and leadership coaching and training face-to-face and online.

CONFLICT COACHING FUNDAMENTALS

Working with Conflict Stories

Samantha Hardy

LONDON AND NEW YORK

First published 2022
by Routledge
2 Park Square, Milton Park, Abingdon, Oxon OX14 4RN

and by Routledge
605 Third Avenue, New York, NY 10158

Routledge is an imprint of the Taylor & Francis Group, an informa business

© 2022 Samantha Hardy

British Library Cataloguing-in-Publication Data
A catalogue record for this book is available from the British Library

Library of Congress Cataloging-in-Publication Data
Names: Hardy, Samantha, author.
Title: Conflict coaching fundamentals : working with conflict stories /
Samantha Hardy | Identifiers: LCCN 2021008962 (print) |
LCCN 2021008963 (ebook) | ISBN 9780367651428 (hbk) |
ISBN 9780367651442 (pbk) | ISBN 9781003128038 (ebk)
Subjects: LCSH: Conflict management. | Interpersonal relations.
Classification: LCC HM1126 .H37 2022 (print) | LCC HM1126 (ebook) |
DDC 303.6/9--dc23
LC record available at https://lccn.loc.gov/2021008962
LC ebook record available at https://lccn.loc.gov/2021008963

ISBN: 978-0-367-65142-8 (hbk)
ISBN: 978-0-367-65144-2 (pbk)
ISBN: 978-1-003-12803-8 (ebk)

DOI: 10.4324/9781003128038

Typeset in Joanna
by Deanta Global Publishing Services, Chennai, India

CONTENTS

FIGURES

TABLE

AUTHOR BIOGRAPHY

Samantha Hardy is the principal and lead trainer at CCI Academy, an organisation that provides coaching and training in conflict management and leadership.

Sam began her working career as a litigation lawyer but, since being certified as a Community Mediator in 1997, has focused on providing mediation and coaching to support people in resolving their conflicts. She has been accredited under the Australian National Mediator Approval System and by the U.S. Institute of Conflict Transformation as a Certified Transformative Mediator. She is a Certified Narrative Coach and the founder of the REAL Conflict Coaching System™.

Sam is also a well-known university educator, holding adjunct appointments at various universities in Australia, Hong Kong, Singapore and the USA. She is an affiliate scholar at the Center for the Study of Narrative and Conflict Resolution within the Carter School for Peace and Conflict Resolution at George Mason University in Washington, DC.

In 2021 Sam was awarded the Resolution Institute Award for Service to Dispute Resolution in Australia for her leadership and innovation in the dispute resolution sphere, with continuous focus and dedication towards both practitioners and academics.

Sam has undergraduate and postgraduate degrees in law, arts (psychology and French), and education, as well as a PhD in law and conflict resolution.

Sam has published widely, including many articles in academic journals and her books *Dispute Resolution in Australia*, 3rd edition (2014) co-authored with David Spencer; *Mediation for Lawyers* (2010) co-authored with Olivia Rundle; and *Sex, Gender, Sexuality and the Law: Social and Legal Issues Facing Individuals, Couples and Families* (2016) co-authored with Olivia Rundle and Damien Riggs.

ACKNOWLEDGEMENTS

This book began in my PhD research and then developed in the following 20 years based on my experience in practice. During this time so many people have contributed to the ideas developed in this book.

The late Professor Jerome Bruner inspired my interest in the connection between narratives and our life experiences. I was fortunate enough to spend an entire day with him talking about my research and receiving a great deal of encouragement and feedback from him during my PhD candidature. He was incredibly generous with his time and suggestions.

My PhD supervisor Professor Dirk Meure was also incredibly important in the development of my early ideas around melodrama and tragedy and provided a great deal of theoretical and moral support!

Various colleagues have contributed to my thinking, not least of whom is my friend and colleague Professor Nadja Alexander, with whom I developed the REAL Conflict Coaching System.

Other colleagues who provided a great deal of feedback on early drafts of the book include Judith Rafferty, Olivia Rundle, and Claudia Butler.

Much of the manuscript was written during my time as a visiting scholar at the Center for Narrative and Conflict Resolution at George Mason University in Washington, DC. I am grateful to Professor Sara Cobb for the invitation to visit and her consistent interest in and support of my work. I also appreciated many fascinating discussions with Alison Castel and Sarah Federman during my time there.

Finally, I thank all of my students and clients for sharing their conflict stories with me and for prompting so much reflective practice with their questions and comments.

PREFACE

I like to think of myself as a pracademic; that is, a combination of a practitioner and an academic. For more than 20 years I have worked, taught, and researched in the field of conflict management and resolution. I provide a range of consultancy services including mediation and conflict management coaching. I also conduct conflict management training, through universities and for private organisations, both in person and online. I also conduct research and write articles and books about conflict management.

I started my career as a litigation lawyer. Fresh out of university, being in court seemed very exciting! I loved advocating for my clients and working to persuade a judge that my client's case was the strongest. After a few years, though, I started to feel a bit disillusioned. Even when my clients won (and sometimes that meant receiving a HUGE payout!) they frequently seemed unhappy with the whole process and the outcome. It took me a while to understand why.

In 1997 I completed a Master of Laws, studying at night and on weekends while working full time. One of the last subjects I studied was called "Alternative Dispute Resolution" and was all about using processes other than going to court to resolve conflicts. I learnt about the different elements of conflict and how legal processes usually ignored most of these, focusing instead on fairly narrowly defined "legal issues". I started to realise that the main reason my clients were unhappy, even when they had "won", was that many of the aspects of the conflict that were important to them were not resolved, or even discussed, in the legal proceedings.

Students who completed the Alternative Dispute Resolution subject were given the option to undertake an additional two-day training to receive certification as a community mediator, and I jumped at this opportunity.

The training for me was a kind of epiphany! Alternative dispute resolution allowed people to address all elements of their conflict, without the stressful, time-consuming, and costly process of going to court. More important, it allowed people to take control of their own conflict resolution process – to participate, be heard, and make their own choices – instead of their conflict being taken over by lawyers and their future being decided upon by some old guy in a grey wig!

I was hooked! Mediation was what I wanted to do! The problem was that at that time, it was nearly impossible to make a living as a mediator. Mediation wasn't as mainstream as it is today and was often provided as a voluntary service through community organisations. But I was now on a mission!

I quit my job as a lawyer (much to the horror of my family and friends). I was offered a PhD fellowship at a local university, which provided me with some income while I completed a PhD in return for my teaching some classes in the law school.

In my PhD, I interviewed people who had experienced conflict. Actually, I didn't really "interview" them as such, in that I didn't ask too many questions. Instead, what I asked them to do was simply "tell me what happened" and then, when they had finished telling me their story, I asked them whether they had seen a lawyer about the matter. My original theory had been that the people who had seen lawyers were more likely to talk about their conflict in an adversarial way, but in the end this became a chicken/egg type problem – did the people who told their conflict more adversarially do so because they'd talked with a lawyer, or were the people who told their story in that way more likely to go see a lawyer in the first place? I couldn't figure out a way to answer those questions.

What I did discover, though, is that there are two very typical "types" of stories that people tell when they are in conflict. There's the kind of story that people tell when they are not managing their conflict well, when they feel stuck and helpless and want someone to save them. And then, there's the kind of story that people tell when they are actively engaging in improving their conflict situation – when they are the hero of their own story. I also realised that there are things that we can do to help people to develop the "stuck/helpless" story that they are telling themselves, so that they can become proactive and take steps to improve their conflict situation.

From this starting point, and over many years of working with people in conflict both as a mediator and as coach, I developed a conflict coaching model that for many years was known as "Sam's working model". Professor Nadja Alexander, my colleague and friend, helped me to refine it into what is now known as the REAL Conflict Coaching System. This system is designed to be a simple and intuitive guide to support people to more deeply reflect on their conflict and to identify and evaluate a range of choices for moving forward. It supports people to develop their competence and confidence to manage their own conflict more effectively.

My mission in life is to work towards a more peaceful future for everyone. My main focus is on the workplace, because work takes up a large part of our lives and research is showing that individual conflict and dissatisfaction in the workplace are increasing dramatically. My practice experience leads me to believe that a big part of this problem is because many managers do not have the competence or the confidence to manage conflict effectively. They are well-intentioned but have not had the opportunity to develop the skills that they need to deal with conflict early and proactively. I want to change this!

This book is designed primarily for people who support others in conflict, whether as a private conflict management consultant or as a manager or human resources practitioner within an organisational setting. However, the book will also be useful to people as individuals, in that it will provide insight into the stories that we tell ourselves about our conflicts and perhaps inspire some critical self-reflection about our own conflict stories and how they help or hinder our management of the situation. It will also provide some insight into the stories told by our friends, family members, and colleagues and perhaps allow you to support them better in an informal way as they invite you into their stories.

INTRODUCTION

In both my work as a conflict management specialist and my private life, people tell me their conflict stories all the time. People in conflict frequently talk about it with others (although usually not with the person or people with whom they are in conflict). Sharing our conflict stories may be driven by a need to vent our emotions, clarify in our own minds what is going on and why it bothers us, seek assistance and advice, or a combination of these things.

Conflict stories may be told after the conflict has been resolved or in the middle of the conflict. In this book I will focus on the stories told by people in conflict that has not been resolved. They are the stories of people who come seeking assistance with their conflict, so the audience is someone like a manager, a lawyer, a mediator, or a conflict coach. In this context, the storyteller is not an omniscient narrator or observer of the conflict. Rather, the storyteller is a character – in fact, the main character – in the story they tell. They bring you the story unfinished. In fact, the main reason they come to conflict specialists is because they want closure – a particular type of closure usually – so that they can end the story and move on.

Though every conflict story has its own particular context, characters, and complexities, in some ways they are all the same. This is because humans are programmed to talk about conflict in a particular way. In my experience and research, I have discovered that what many conflict stories have in common is that they tend to be melodramatic in their content and structure. Melodramatic stories are comforting in their familiar form, by always clearly distinguishing between the "goodies" and the "baddies" and by resolving with a happy ending. However, real life is more complex and doesn't work like a melodramatic plot. The more we tell ourselves melodramatic stories about conflict, the more likely we are to be disappointed and unprepared to manage the real-life situation.

The problem with melodramatic conflict stories is that they encourage the storyteller to simplify the plot. We want to try to keep everything as straightforward as possible, so we look like the "good guy" and it appears clear what the solution should be (usually some version of the bad guy being punished and the good guy being rewarded). Though this all sounds good in theory, reality is never quite this straightforward. Conflict situations are usually more complex, and "dream justice" is not usually available or even the best possible outcome.

Importantly, this tendency to adopt a simplistic melodramatic plotline distracts us from important information that might be useful for us in managing the situation more constructively. The storyteller must also cast themselves in the innocent victim role – this implicitly encourages the storyteller to ignore their own contributions to the conflict and to remain passive and helpless in the situation. Melodramatic stories discourage us from recognising that there may have been different choices that we could have made in the past and prevent us from identifying choices that might be available to us in the future that might improve the situation. Melodrama is also premised on an "all or nothing" mentality, in which we either win or lose and in which the outcome is reverting to an idealised past. There is no room for incremental improvement, let alone working towards something better than what existed in the past.

In my work with clients in conflict, I spend time assisting them to draw out the complexity of the situations they are facing. We explore everybody's actions and intentions and recognise other possible interpretations of events. We specifically focus on the "grey" areas in the story, the gaps and the paradoxes. We discuss the impact of the situation on everyone concerned, and we look for opportunities for choice and action. I help my clients find a balance between optimistic and realistic. In summary, my goal is to support them to change from being a melodramatic victim to becoming the active hero of their conflict story!

In this book I explore how people in conflict construct their stories about their experience of conflict and the meanings they make from these stories. I also take into account the social aspect of telling such conflict stories – including the anticipated audience, what the storyteller expects from them in response to the story, and the impact of the particular form of storytelling on the people involved in the conflict. The book includes examples of many conflict stories told by people I have interviewed as part of my research and others told by my clients and students. Their names have been changed and in some cases their stories have been edited or combined to protect their confidentiality.

I suggest that there is a particular kind of conflict narrative (a kind of master story or template) typically adopted by people in conflict who are not managing the conflict well and also that there is a better, but less typical, form of conflict narrative that is more conducive to constructive conflict management. I explain how the typical dysfunctional conflict narrative fits the genre of melodrama and explore the different characters who populate the melodramatic narrative and the development of the melodramatic plot. I also demonstrate how the typical melodramatic conflict narrative structures and distorts people's experience of conflict and actually makes it harder for them to constructively engage with, manage, and resolve the conflict. I also suggest, somewhat counterintuitively, that a more constructive conflict narrative has many of the attributes of the genre of tragedy, although with clients I work on developing "tragedy with a twist", using the depth and reflection of the tragic hero to develop a more positive outcome than is typically associated with tragedy.

Part 1 of the book explores the nature of melodramatic conflict stories, their plots and their characters, and the problems that they create for people in conflict moving forwards. After reading the first few chapters, you will not listen to people talking about their conflicts in the same way ever again! You will also become more self-reflective about the conflict stories that you tell yourself and others. You are going to notice patterns in the stories that people tell and be able to identify areas in their conflict stories that are likely to be open to exploration and improvement. You will understand how conflict stories can work against us effectively managing and resolving conflict. You will also learn about the main shifts that people in conflict need to make to escape from the melodrama of conflict and develop their stories into one of learning and growth.

Part 2 of the book introduces the role of the coach as a means to support people to escape from their entrapment in a melodramatic conflict story and to become the active hero of their future. You will learn how to be careful about the role you play in another person's conflict story, to ensure that you don't become part of the problem! You will discover the six main shifts that a conflict story needs to make to build a person's capacity to manage the conflict more effectively, now and into the future.

Throughout the book, I use the word "client" to refer to the person in conflict, but I acknowledge that a form of conflict coaching may occur outside a professional coach/client relationship. For example, managers may coach a member of their team, parents may coach their children, colleagues and friends may coach one another. We might even coach ourselves through a process of self-reflection!

Part 1

CONFLICT STORIES

1

CONFLICT STORIES, NARRATIVE, AND GENRE

Human beings are predisposed to creating stories as a way of making sense of the world. In fact, Jonathan Gottshall (2013), author of *The Storytelling Animal: How Stories Make Us Human*, suggests that our addiction to stories is the defining attribute that makes us successful as a species. Sharing stories is a way for people to form community and cultural bonds. Stories also provide a way for us to practice social skills and rehearse our responses to real-life challenges. They encourage us to behave ethically, by teaching us about good and evil and the consequences of our choices. However, our tendency to default to certain kinds of stories can also create problems, particularly in situations of conflict.

Human beings frequently create stories, even if information is limited or there is no story there. We invent one that provides some meaning to what may objectively be an abstract collection of phenomena. This story creation habit was demonstrated perfectly in a famous experiment conducted by two psychologists in the mid-1940s. Fritz Heider and Marianne Simmel (1944) conducted an experiment in which they showed 114 people a short,

DOI: 10.4324/9781003128038-1

abstract, animated film with some geometric shapes moving around a screen. An image from the film can be seen in Figure 1.1.

They asked their subjects to describe what they saw. Almost all of the viewers (111 of the 114 participants) described what they saw in the form of a story: doors slamming, courtship dances, the foiling of a predator. Their responses not only described the movement of the shapes but also gave each shape a human character with a personality and motives to explain its movement on the screen.

When it comes to human interactions, we have the same tendency to script stories that create meaning far beyond our actual observations. In many cases, this story creation is useful and leads to shared understanding without the need for complex communication. For example, when I say to my friend, "Gosh my head hurts, I had a big night last night!" she is likely to understand that I went out with friends, had a few too many alcoholic drinks, and have a headache because I'm hungover. I don't need to provide all of the graphic details for her to understand the story. It's a familiar kind of story that she recognises and she can join the dots. The context in which I tell the story, and my chosen audience, may also impact the "standard story" that is used to interpret my abbreviated version of events. For example, if I was talking to another parent in my new parents' group, their interpretation of my statement may be that my baby didn't sleep well and neither did I!

However, our tendency to create stories based on incomplete information is more than an academic exercise or a fast-tracked way for people

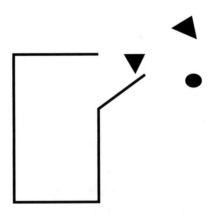

Figure 1.1 Image from Heider Simmel experiment

to communicate. In some situations, our tendency to create stories from limited information can lead to problems. Frank (2010), in his wonderful book *Letting Stories Breathe*, explains that stories give form to lives that inherently lack form. In other words, stories provide us with a way of organising our experiences into a coherent structure providing temporal and spatial orientation, meaning, intention, and boundaries. Frank cautions that how stories inform lives can be a gift or a danger. This is because stories have the power to affect what people are able to see as real, as possible, and as worth doing or best avoided. Frank describes how people can become deeply caught up in one version of a story, even though the same events could be told to a very different effect, and how people may feel compelled to act out what the story requires.

Gottshall (2013) gives the example of conspiracy theories as one kind of problem story. He describes a conspiracy theory as a fictional story connecting real information and imagined information into a coherent and emotionally satisfying version of reality. Gottshall (2013) says:

> Conspiracy theories offer ultimate answers to a great mystery of the human condition: why are things so bad in the world? They provide nothing less than a solution to the problem of evil. In the imaginative world of the conspiracy theorist, there is no accidental badness. To the conspiratorial mind, shit never just happens. History is not just one damned thing after another, and only dopes and sheeple believe in coincidences. For this reason, conspiracy theories – no matter how many devils they invoke – are always consoling in their simplicity. Bad things do not happen because of a widely complex swirl of abstract historical and social variables. They happen because bad men live to stalk our happiness. And you can fight, and possibly even defeat, bad men. ... (116)

He notes that conspiracy theories are not just about grand topics such as aliens, or 9/11. We all have our own personal conspiracy theories about things that happen in our daily lives.

In many ways, the kinds of stories we tell ourselves about conflict typically have the attributes of conspiracy theories. They tend to connect real and imagined information into a form that seems coherent and emotionally satisfying. They blame others (the bad guy) for causing our suffering, and they lead us to believe that a certain kind of justice (usually based on the bad guy receiving his comeuppance) is right and available. The problem is, however, that these stories are not complete, they are not "true" for everyone involved, they are based on many assumptions, and they often make it more difficult to improve our situation by narrowing our thinking and our options.

Conflict stories and narratives

In this book, you will discover that not only are our conflict stories typically based on incomplete information and plenty of assumptions, they are also structured around a common kind of master story or narrative[1] that limits our understanding and possible responses to the situation. Jerome Bruner (2002) notes that it is only "when we suspect we have the wrong story that we begin asking how a narrative may structure (or distort) our view of how things really are" (24). Professionals who work with clients in conflict (and perhaps everyone who hears stories from their colleagues, friends, and family members about their conflicts) will recognise certain repetitive patterns in the many conflict stories to which they have been an audience. They will also acknowledge the potentially dysfunctional nature of many conflict stories and how these tend to perpetuate the conflict. There is a growing interest in the intersection between conflict and narrative, as evidenced by the work of Kenneth Cloke (2000), John Winslade and Gerald Monk (2008; Monk and Winslade, 2012), Sara Cobb (1994, 2013), and Solon Simmons (2020).

For many people in conflict, their reality does not meet the expectations of their story – they end up extremely frustrated, because their desired ending (what they see as justice) seems elusive, if not impossible. And yet, the typical structure of such conflict stories is pervasive and persistent. In this book, you will discover what is common in those repetitive patterns (the underlying narrative that provides the foundation for the individual stories) and develop a framework to explore and break away from the limitations of that narrative.

Genre and conflict stories

For my PhD research, I interviewed people who had suffered an injury as a result of someone else's actions. In one sense, I didn't really *interview* them because I did not ask them a sequence of predesigned questions. Rather, I simply asked them to tell me what happened and recorded their response. Inevitably, my participants told me a story. As I reviewed the stories I had collected, I found that there were two distinct types of stories (two different master narratives), one in which the person told a story of learning and growth and another in which the story was one of injustice and suffering.

Coincidentally, at the time I was trying to come up with a methodology to analyse the two different kinds of conflict narratives, I was studying a university subject on French literature. One of the required readings for the course was the Pixérécourt melodrama *Coelina* (Holcroft, 1824; discussed further in Chapter 2). As I read the script I was struck by its similarities to the "injustice and suffering" stories of my research subjects. This led to my researching the genre of melodrama in more detail and identifying some very strong connections between that genre and many of the conflict stories that I had collected. My dilemma, then, was to find a genre that mapped onto the other "learning and growth" stories, and after much research, to my surprise I found that the genre of tragedy was the best fit (I know this seems counterintuitive, because tragedy seems like a negative kind of genre to use, but stick with me and later in the book I'll explain why it's actually quite useful). Considering conflict stories through these two genres provides a great deal of insight as to where (and why) those stories are more or less helpful in motivating the storyteller to take constructive steps to manage their conflict.

Genre can help identify what Baruch Bush and Folger (1994) call "an underlying orientation to conflict" (8) and can provide a framework for exploring the way in which these orientations are driven by broad ideologies about social relations and social intervention. Baruch Bush and Folger (1994) explain that the stories people tell about conflict "carry implicit notions of what conflict is and expectations about what moves or responses are possible or required in specific contexts, what role third parties play, and what outcomes are desirable" (8). Exploring conflict stories through genre draws our attention specifically to character roles and positioning of the parties and typical plotlines and themes and how these work together to promote coherence. Creating coherence is particularly important because, as Cobb (1994) explains, coherence provides stability and seals off discursive sites where meaning could be contested. In other words, when a story is too neat and tidy, it stops us from investigating the situation further and lulls us into a false sense of righteousness and security.

Genre also provides a tool to examine the process of telling stories in the conflict context. Stories of a particular genre may be told only in certain situations, and certain situations invoke the telling of a particular genre of stories. For example, it may be perfectly acceptable to tell the story of the latest conflict you've had with your spouse to your best friend, whereas it's not so acceptable to launch into the same story with a stranger you happen to sit next to on the bus. Similarly, in the context of your new parents' group, telling each other the stories of your birth experience is almost expected, but it would be inappropriate at your business networking event. Accordingly, an analysis of the content of a particular genre of story is incomplete without exploring the context in which it is likely to be told. This includes a consideration of factors such as the status of the storyteller, the intended audience, and the purpose for which the story is told in those circumstances.

In the following chapters we will explore the two genres I identified as corresponding to the "injustice and suffering" stories (melodrama) and the "learning and growth" stories (tragedy) that I collected from people in conflict. We will examine how those different genres tend to either narrow or expand our thinking about conflict and how they affect our capacity to manage it. We will then consider ways to support people who are stuck in an "injustice and suffering" story to develop their thinking into a "learning and growth" story, thus opening up opportunities for them to better manage their own future.

Note

1   Though many writers use the terms "story" and "narrative" interchangeably, in this book I adopt Baron and Epstein's (1997) distinction between the two terms. A story is "an individual account of an event or set of events that unfolds over time and whose beginning, middle, and end are intended to resolve (or question the possibility of resolving) the problem set in motion at the start" (147–148). Narrative is a broader concept, a kind of cumulative version of the key features of a group of similar stories that represents their aggregate meaning. The concept of narrative also includes consideration of how such stories are produced and received so that what they say about the problems they deal with is culturally meaningful to both narrator and audience.

REFERENCES

Baron, J. B. and Epstein, J. 1997. Is law narrative? *Buffalo Law Review* 45(1): 141–187.

Baruch Bush, R. A. and Folger, J. P. 1994. *The promise of mediation: responding to conflict through empowerment and recognition.* San Francisco: Jossey-Bass.

Bruner, J. 2002. *Making stories: law, literature, life.* Cambridge, MA: Harvard University Press.

Cloke, K. 2000. *Resolving personal and organizational conflict: stories of transformation and forgiveness.* Wiley.

Cobb, S. 1994. A narrative perspective on mediation: toward the materialization of the storytelling metaphor. In Folger, J. P. and Jones, T. S. (Eds.), *New directions in mediation: communication research and perspectives*, pp. 48–66. Thousand Oaks, CA: Sage.

Cobb, S. 2013. *Speaking of violence: the politics and poetics of narrative in conflict resolution.* Oxford University Press.

Frank, A. W. 2010. *Letting stories breathe: a socio-narratology.* Chicago: University of Chicago Press.

Gottschall, J. 2013. *The storytelling animal: how stories make us human.* New York: Houghton Mifflin Harcourt.

Heider, F. and Simmel, M. 1944. An experimental study of apparent behavior. *The American Journal of Psychology* 57: 243–259.

Holcroft, T. (Trans.). 1824. A tale of mystery. (Original publication Guilbert de Pixérécourt, R.-C. 1800. *Coelina: ou l'enfant de mystère.* London: John Cumberland.)

Monk, G. and Winslade, J. 2012. *When stories clash: addressing conflict with narrative mediation.* Taos Institute Publishers.

Simmons, S. 2020. *Root narrative theory and conflict resolution: power, justice and values.* Routledge.

Winslade, J. and Monk, G. 2008. *Practising narrative mediation: loosening the grip of conflict.* John Wiley & Sons.

2

MELODRAMA

In this chapter we will consider the genre of melodrama, examining its traditional characters and typical plot. As you read about how melodramatic stories were historically played out on the stage, see if you can identify some parallels with modern conflict stories and think about why this genre might be so prevalent in the conflict stories we tell ourselves and others. In the next chapter (Chapter 3) we will see why the genre of melodrama is so conducive to conflict stories and examine how melodramatic conflict stories create individual and societal expectations about conflict and how we should manage it.

What is melodrama?

In everyday conversation, we frequently use the word "melodrama" as a kind of derogatory term indicating that something is overly dramatic and unrealistic (as in "Don't be so melodramatic!"). Though sensationalism and overwrought emotion are certainly attributes of many melodramatic plays and movies, the genre in a literary sense has other important

DOI: 10.4324/9781003128038-2

characteristics. Another commonly understood meaning of melodrama is that it is a kind of musical theatre, with songs and music accompanying the action. Obviously, that definition is not particularly helpful when applying the genre to modern conflict stories, because people don't usually play out their conflict with a musical soundtrack! For the purposes of this book, we will define melodrama broadly as a story with a sensational and improbable plot that focuses on the suffering of a main virtuous character at the hands of an evil villain. The plot focuses on actions, not character development, and virtue always wins over evil in the end. The genre is designed to elicit strong emotions from the audience and to leave the audience satisfied that justice has been done by the end of the story.

Melodrama originated in France around the time of the French Revolution. French playwright Pixérécourt is generally accepted as the "father" of the genre. His play Coelina: ou l'enfant de mystère, translated as Coelina, or The Child of Mystery (Holcroft, 1824), was first produced at the Théâtre de l'Ambigu-Comique on 2 September 1800. Coelina is the play most often associated with the birth of French melodrama and the melodramatic genre. Based on a popular novel by Ducray-Duminil, it is a story about an orphaned girl, Coelina, who is in the care of her ward, Dufour, the brother of Coelina's supposed father. Coelina is in love with Dufour's son Stephany, and he loves her in return. However, Truguelin, the brother of Coelina's deceased mother, is a wicked man who plots to gain control of Coelina's inheritance by arranging a marriage between her and his son. When Truguelin's plans are thwarted, he reveals that Dufour's brother was not, in fact, Coelina's father. As it turns out, her real father is Francisque, an impoverished mute man who has been sheltering at Dufour's house. At this news, Dufour declares Coelina a "child of adultery" and banishes her and Francisque from his home. For the remainder of the play Dufour attempts to unravel the confusion and find out the truth about Coelina's parentage. In the end (spoiler alert!) Dufour discovers that Coelina's mother was secretly married to Francisque and so Coelina's legitimacy of birth is established. Dufour also discovers that it was Truguelin who cut out Francisque's tongue as part of his evil plan to steal Coelina's inheritance. Truguelin is banished, Coelina's marriage to Stephany takes place, and everyone (except for Truguelin) lives happily ever after.[1]

Melodramatic theatre was entertainment for the working classes. Singer (2001) suggests that it was a response to the post-Revolution condition of individual vulnerability and competitive individualism within capitalist modernity. Melodrama aimed to inspire a sense of security and comfort about the controllability and predictability of a complex world in times of change and uncertainty.

Melodrama's characters

Characters in melodrama are monopathic. In other words, they are always consistent in their personality and actions. They are essentially stereotypes and abstractions without complexity, internal inconsistencies, or inner conflict. Any conflict in melodrama is between the characters, rather than internal. There are only two types of characters in melodrama – good characters and evil characters – and they are easily identifiable right from the start of the story. Good characters are sweet and kind and attractive, and bad characters are evil and scheming and ugly. Good characters demonstrate only virtuous conduct, and bad characters perform despicable actions. They never behave out of character.

People in melodrama are true to their superficial appearance and consistently think and behave in the same way. They are never indecisive and do not need to worry about making choices – the course of action is always obvious because it is what a "good" or a "bad" character would do in such a situation. Accordingly, melodrama is all about action and is not concerned about psychological complexity or character development. The audience focuses on what the characters do, and their intention goes without saying based on whether they are good or evil – good characters always do things with good intentions and evil characters are always motivated by bad intentions.

The two main characters in melodrama, who are diametrically opposed, are the heroine (the main virtuous character) and the villain (the main evil character). There are two other characters, the father figure and the heroine's bumbling helper, both of whom are virtuous characters.

The heroine

The heroine (illustrated in Figure 2.1) is the main character in melodrama, and the story is told from her perspective. Melodramatic heroines are stereotypically feminine: innocent, passive, and helpless. They are dependent on male characters for their well-being and security.

Figure 2.1 The melodramatic heroine

The heroine is the embodiment of virtue. She is as morally strong as she is physically fragile and weak. In the typical melodramatic plot, the heroine's virtue is called into question by the villain and she experiences extreme suffering as a result. The heroine is dependent on the father figure to recognise her virtue, punish the villain, and restore the heroine to her rightful place (this is known as the father figure providing "dream justice").

Melodramatic heroines are acted upon rather than being active themselves. They respond to suffering with passivity. The innocent heroine under difficulty frequently succumbs to a melodramatic despair of the world and demonstrates a sense of the hopelessness of things (Heilman, 1968). The passive nature of the heroine is often demonstrated by her muteness, which is symbolic of the defencelessness of innocence (Brooks, 1976). The heroine's muteness is often metaphoric or representative; for example, the heroine is from another culture and cannot be understood, she has taken a vow of silence, or she is locked away in a dungeon where nobody can hear her cries for help. The melodramatic heroine needs someone else to act and speak for her in order to have her virtue recognised and her suffering alleviated.

In classical melodrama, the heroine never actively attempts to solve the problem created by the villain. She simply resists by continuing to demonstrate her virtuous nature and waiting for other more authoritative characters to recognise it and rescue her. Coelina, for example, does not take steps to investigate the true circumstances of her birth. Surprisingly, she does not even ask Francisque to explain things to her during their journey away from Dufour's home. In fact, Francisque only reveals his marriage to her mother when asked by Dufour some time later.

The villain

In melodrama, the villain (almost always male, illustrated in Figure 2.2) is the embodiment of evil. He is recognisable the minute he walks on stage; he is the swarthy, cape-enveloped man with a deep voice. He commits only acts of evil and does so suitably dressed. The villain's motives are always immoral: he is ambitious, greedy, jealous, or lustful. He covets something that he does not deserve. He pursues his desires with relentless single-mindedness. The villain usually proceeds in his plans with some clear advantage over the other characters (and particularly the heroine). He

Figure 2.2 The evil villain

may have greater physical, financial, or social power, which he uses for his villainous purposes. The motivation for his actions is usually portrayed as disproportionate to the quantity of the villainy unleashed. He may murder for a small amount of money, destroy an entire village because one resident has insulted him, or ruin an entire family because the daughter does not return his affections. This lack of proportion helps in his characterisation as truly evil, because the less motivation can be demonstrated, the more the villain's actions appear volitional and unjustified.

Despite the villain's very active pursuit of his goals and the power base that he exploits for this purpose, in the end he always receives his comeuppance. Good always triumphs over evil.

The father figure

In melodrama, those with responsibility for restoring the moral order when the villain usurps it are the older generation of virtuous males. The father figure in melodrama (illustrated in Figure 2.3) is the person with primary responsibility or power to protect the heroine. He is often the heroine's actual father or guardian but may also be a larger scale patriarch such as a military ruler, a king, or a judge. It is the father figure who must actively recognise the heroine's innocence and virtue, punish the villain for his evil deeds, and put things right again. The father figure directs other characters to assist him in his task and is the final decision maker when the time comes for "dream justice" to be implemented. The heroine's destiny is ultimately in his hands.

The bumbling helper

The heroine in melodrama is often supported by a bumbling helper (illustrated in Figure 2.4). He is virtuous and well-intentioned but practically useless. He is completely on the heroine's side (often he is her devoted and dependable sweetheart) and tends to make long speeches about the virtues of his beloved. He is generally a passive character, although when he does take action he is usually outwitted by the villain. The bumbling helper is confused and extraordinarily gullible, although his flaws are always forgiven because his heart is in the right place.

Figure 2.3 The father figure

The melodramatic plot

Classical melodramatic plots usually consist of three acts: the first demonstrates the good characters in a state of virtue and happiness; the second involves the "primal scene" in which this state comes under threat due to the actions of the villain; and the final act is the scene of the trial, in which virtue and vice are recognised, the villain gets his comeuppance, and virtue is rewarded ("dream justice" is achieved).

Figure 2.4 The bumbling helper

The melodramatic plot has a number of attributes that contribute to this basic structure. Firstly, the storyline is overly simplistic, particularly in relation to causal linkages between the characters, their actions, and problematic outcomes. This simplification ensures that the story is coherent, because many of the hidden complexities undermine the convincing nature of the path to dream justice.

Blame is individualised and moralised. It is always the villain's deliberate actions that cause the heroine's suffering. When other characters are generally quite passive in response to the villain's activity, it is easy to focus blame on the villain. This focus on the actions of the villain also allows the good characters (and the audience, who relate to them) to identify all suffering with an external cause. Good characters never need to consider their own responsibility or contribution to the situation. Heilman (1968) explains: "If the disaster comes from human evil, it is the evil of others, not ourselves: we are innocent, and we can grieve, if we wish, instead of looking more steadily at ourselves" (35).

For example, in Coelina, Truguelin is portrayed as wholly responsible for Coelina's suffering, due to his actions in forcing Coelina's mother to undergo a second sham marriage and then concealing this fact. Although Truguelin is clearly blameworthy to some extent for these actions, it is overly simplistic to say that Coelina's subsequent difficulties are solely caused by him. There are other characters in the play who have the opportunity to avoid or at least lessen Coelina's suffering, had they chosen to take certain actions. For example, it is arguable that Coelina's mother could have refused to go ahead with the second sham marriage in the first place. Or, alternatively, she could have told Coelina the truth about her real father's identity before she died. Coelina's real father, Francisque, could also have disclosed what he knew at an earlier time. Coelina's guardian, Dufour, could have followed his heart and made further enquiries, rather than initially taking Truguelin at his word.

Melodrama's focus on the villain also diverts attention from some larger societal issues underlying the plot. For example, Coelina's suffering may be said to have been caused by the traditional view that being an illegitimate child (born to people who are not married) was a nonvirtuous state. In other words, society treated people who were born illegitimately as not deserving of certain benefits due to virtuous members of society. Coelina's suffering may also be said to have been caused by that society's requirement that women be dependent on their father/guardian and their husband for their well-being. These systemic problems are obscured by the simplification of the issue of blame as between the heroine and the villain.

Melodrama thus ignores history and context and simply assumes that there is a clear starting point to the conflict, usually some action by the villain. Blame is a fundamental sentiment in melodrama. Heilman (1968) describes blame as a "moral sedative" (129), suggesting that everyone wants to feel right, and one of the ways to do this is to point the finger at those who do wrong. In melodrama characters are either in total defence or attack mode.

The audience is encouraged to identify with the good characters and to hate the evil characters. The emotions elicited by melodrama towards its characters are often extreme. Melodrama is designed to arouse a kind of primal bloodlust (Singer, 2001) in which the audience hates the villain so intensely that they want him extinguished. This hatred stems from a feeling of moral injustice, because in melodrama the main role of the villain is to cause the heroine extreme suffering.

The heroine's suffering results in the audience feeling pity and sadness for her. Aristotle defined this kind of emotional response to a person's suffering as "pathos". Importantly, pathos is based on the premise that the person suffering did not deserve it and also that the audience can relate to the suffering as something that they might imagine could happen to themselves. Heilman (1968) describes melodrama as incorporating a sense of "innocence neurosis" (114) in which the victim never deserves her fate and (along with the audience) finds it irrational and untimely.

The melodramatic plot also tends to rely on exaggeration, outrageous coincidence, implausibility, and convoluted plotting (Singer, 2001). However, the focus on the evil villain and his actions provides a fictional certainty leading to the final dream justice. Dream justice involves a very public recognition of the heroine's virtue and the villain's moral failings. It is the stereotypical "happy ending" where the audience can enjoy the seductive pleasures of melodramatic wholeness without considering the effects on those outside the simplified narrative or acknowledging alternatives (Smith, 1973).

In melodrama, dream justice implements a return to the idealised past. The villain is presented as having upset the moral order, the way things should be, and dream justice restores the damage, punishes the villain, and allows life to continue as if the villain's actions had not occurred. Despite the comforting fantasy of dream justice, Nowell-Smith (1977) reminds us that "melodrama's happy end is often impossible, and, what is more, the audience knows it is impossible" (117). Dream justice is impossible for a number of reasons. Firstly, it is based on an overly simplistic and unrealistic version of events. Secondly, the past can never be fully restored nor the villain's actions entirely undone. The heroine has suffered, and at least the memory of that suffering remains.

Finally, a related problem with dream justice is that it focuses on restoring the status quo – there is no room for change, improvement, or growth. The audience is never encouraged to challenge or question the underlying social structures or contextual factors that have been repressed in the simplified plot.

Though the everyday conflicts we experience at work and at home do not usually end up the subject of highly dramatic theatrical productions, when we fail to manage our conflicts well we often start to adopt some melodramatic characteristics in the story we tell ourselves (and others) about our conflict. In the following chapters we will explore how modern conflict stories tend to fit the melodramatic genre and why this can be so problematic in terms of our ability to manage the conflict effectively.

Note

1 For a modern-day movie melodrama, see the film *Slumdog Millionaire* (Colson, 2008), in which an innocent teenage orphan, about to win a staggering amount of money on a television game show, is accused of cheating. The story follows the police inspector's attempt to assess his virtue. Will he be found to be truthful and be allowed to answer the final question, perhaps win 20 million rupees, and even find the girl he loves? This film doesn't quite fit the traditional melodrama genre, in that the bad guy of the film is not the main instigator of the challenge to the protagonist's virtue and there is more character development and consideration of societal factors. However, the basic plot of the innocent and vulnerable protagonist suffering when his virtue is challenged and the father figure's quest to evaluate his virtue is very consistent with the genre. Oh, and, of course, there is a happy ending!

REFERENCES

Brooks, P. 1976. *The melodramatic imagination: melodrama and the mode of excess.* New Haven, CT: Yale University Press.

Colson, C. (Producer), Boyle, D. and Tandan, L. (Directors). 2008. *Slumdog millionaire* [Film]. Pathé. Based on the novel by Vikas Swarup.

Heilman, R. B. 1968. *Tragedy and melodrama: versions of experience.* Seattle: University of Washington Press.

Holcroft, T. (Trans.). 1824. A tale of mystery. (Original publication Guilbert de Pixérécourt, R.-C. 1800. *Coelina: ou l'enfant de mystère.* London: John Cumberland.)

Nowell-Smith, G. 1977. Dossier on melodrama: Minelli and melodrama. *Screen* 18(2): 113–118.

Singer, B. 2001. *Melodrama and modernity: early sensational cinema and its contexts*. New York: Columbia University Press.

Smith, J. L. 1973. *Melodrama*. London: Methuen and Co.

3

THE MELODRAMATIC CONFLICT NARRATIVE

Melodramatic conflict stories are not just played out on stage or in novels. People tell them (and enact them) as part of their daily lives. Thinking about the purpose of melodrama as a way to make us more comfortable with change and uncertainty helps us understand why melodrama is such an appealing genre for conflict stories. Conflict is the epitome of change and uncertainty, and it often makes us feel very uncomfortable. When we tell our conflict story to others and we frame it in the genre of melodrama, we feel like the situation is straightforward and the solution is clear, that life has order and is under control. The problem, however, is that melodramatic stories are not realistic and they lull us into a false sense of security and self-righteousness. They also prevent us from managing our conflict constructively.

In later chapters we will consider how the main characters are portrayed in the melodramatic conflict narrative and explore in more detail the impact of the melodramatic form on how we perceive and manage conflict. However, let's first consider how the melodramatic plot looks in a

DOI: 10.4324/9781003128038-3

modern conflict setting and introduce some examples of real conflict stories that fit the melodramatic conflict narrative.

A note about gender

As mentioned in Chapter 2, in classical melodrama, all roles were typically gender specific. The heroine was usually a young woman and the villain was usually a man. They each embodied traditional feminine and masculine qualities, respectively. The heroines were innocent, passive, and dependent; the villains were active and independent.

In the modern conflict narrative, people of all genders may play the heroine role and are also cast in the villain role. Though the character's gender is not as constrained in these real-life stories, the protagonist still needs to demonstrate the stereotypically feminine attributes of innocence, passivity, and dependence on others, and the villain is still portrayed with the stereotypically masculine attributes of activity and independence.

This can make the protagonist role particularly uncomfortable for a man, who has to demonstrate typically feminine qualities to deserve support. Casting oneself in such a role can feel emasculating, particularly in a society in which men are valued for their masculine qualities and discouraged from expressing feminine traits. Two interesting outcomes from this challenge are that (1) men are much less likely to seek support to manage their conflict, because of their resistance to the "heroine" role, and (2) when they do seek support and tell their conflict stories according to the melodramatic conflict narrative, they can be judged harshly compared with women in the same role.

As an experiment, I showed a group of students two videos of people telling their conflict stories. One was a woman; one was a man. Both told a very similar story, and both stories were clearly consistent with the melodramatic conflict narrative. When I asked the students what their reaction was to each of their stories, many students were highly critical of the man. Some described him as "pathetic" and suggested that he should "man up" and "stand up for himself". They found his described passivity and helplessness to be confronting and undesirable. They were much more sympathetic to the woman and expressed that they "felt sorry for her" and "hoped that someone was able to help her".

Students responded in a similar way to the descriptions of the villains in the story. When the villain was described as a man, using less than virtuous means to "win" something over the protagonist, students judged him less harshly than villains who were described as women (students referred to them using terms like "ball-breakers" or "witches"). Men, it seems, were permitted some leeway in their competitive behaviour, or were at least expected to behave in that way, whereas women were judged for promoting their own needs over and above "keeping the peace".

The melodramatic conflict narrative plot

The typical structure of a modern melodramatic conflict narrative looks something like this:

- I am a good person [with context specific examples].
- Life was going well until [villain] came along.
- [Villain] has done x, y, and z to me.
- [Villain] is doing these things deliberately because he is a bad person.
- I am suffering [with sensational language like *nightmare, constant battle*].
- I want it to stop. I want my old life back. I want what I deserve [as a good person].
- There's nothing I can do or say to make this better.
- One of us [the villain or me] has to go.
- Help me please.

Let's consider a few examples of conflict stories that are consistent with the basic plot of the melodramatic conflict narrative. These examples were stories told by real clients in real conflict situations.

Examples of conflict stories

Angela's story

First, let's consider a conflict story told by Angela. This is a transcript of her actual words.

> I have a really bad conflict going on in my life at the moment and I don't know how to deal with it. It's at my workplace. I have this

colleague who has been in this job for 25 years, and she knows, like, in and out of the organisation by her fingertips and she's really good at what she does and in other circumstances I would have got along with her perfectly well, but because I'm a newcomer in this role, I just have trouble dealing with her way of thinking.

She sees me as a threat, which is really discomforting because I don't want to be a threat to anyone, but she believes in experience and that's why she's been in this job for 25 years, and I am straight out of university, I've got two degrees in my hand, and she does not respect that at all because she thinks that experience weighs more than education.

And every day is a constant battle, because I have to prove to her that I'm good in what I'm doing and what I'm going to do, but it's never enough for her, and if I go to her for help, especially regarding my work, she just looks at me and she says, "Don't they teach this at uni?" or, if I do something well, which I think is good, she just says, "Oh, is this all they taught you at uni?"

And everything has the word "university" in it, or my degrees in it, and it clearly shows that she sees me as a threat and it clearly shows that she's threatened by what I have, but at the same time she's trying to make me feel inferior to her, and I don't know how to deal with it because I'm not here to please everyone, but at the same time I can't.
...

Waking up in the morning and going to work is a nightmare right now for me because I don't know how to deal with it.

It's not a happy situation for me, and I think she's enjoying it, because every time she says these things to me she says it with a smirk.

She's the one who did my induction process and she had to show me to my desk where I'll be seated for the rest of the time period of my employment, and the first question she asked me was "Is this fine for you or do you want my desk and chair instead? Do you want my office instead?"

And I just looked at her and ... how do you react to something like that? You think about all these nice smart answers to give back but you don't because at that moment you're in a horrible situation with this person.

And I just stood there looking at her, tongue-tied, didn't know what to say, and I just told her, "It's fine, thank you". I mean, I would have given it back to her but at that moment I was just tongue-tied.

So it's a nightmare, I just don't know what to do. I wish I can get a solution to this, because the only solution I can think of is quit the job, and don't do something which is not making you happy anymore, but do I really have to quit this job for someone who is not worth my time? Or, how do I go ahead with this, because there's absolutely no way I can talk to her about it because she's just going to be like, you know, she's going to ask me, "What, didn't they teach you at uni how to deal with all these things?"

I don't know, I'm just helpless here.

Angela's story review

In Angela's story we see classical elements of melodrama. Angela presents herself as a virtuous employee: she is well-qualified (she has two degrees), and she implies that she usually gets along with people she works with, at least in normal circumstances, and she doesn't want to be a threat to any of her colleagues.

The story is full of dramatic language and is quite sensationalised. Angela, for example, describes her conflict with her colleague as being a "constant battle" and going to work as a "nightmare". Though we should not dismiss Angela's reported feelings as deliberately exaggerated, because she may in fact be suffering a great deal from the situation, we should also not take them on face value – demonstrating extremes of suffering is an important aspect of the melodramatic story. Objectively it seems that having someone frequently comment on your university degrees should not be enough to make going to work so bad that you consider quitting. There is likely to be more going on here than initially disclosed by the client. It is probably more complicated than how Angela has presented it.

She also uses overly inclusive language: "*every* day is a constant battle", "it's *never* enough for her", "*everything* has the word university in it", "*every time* she says these things she says it with a smirk".

The story focuses on the "villain's" actions and how they make Angela suffer. There is very little discussion about anything Angela has done or said. Angela presents herself as the helpless victim of the other woman's actions and mute (she couldn't say anything during the induction conversation, and she can't say anything now to address the situation).

All of the villain's actions are bad, and all are performed with bad intention. There are no examples of good or even neutral interactions between them, and there is no suggestion that at any time the villain's actions are based on anything other than an intention to make Angela suffer.

Similarly, Angela's story is simplified and lacks context. The sequence of events doesn't seem to make sense – there is no history. The first event is the supervisor's statement to her during her induction, and then every conversation they have after that includes the word "university". It seems highly unlikely that the supervisor puts the word "university" into everything she ever says to Angela. It also seems strange that she would make such comments at induction without any history or reason. How, for example, does she know that Angela has two degrees? There are lots of gaps in the story – there are no other characters mentioned, although we can assume that there are other people working there in different roles.

Though Angela doesn't explicitly ask for "dream justice" in the sense that she wants the other woman to receive her comeuppance, she does imply in the way that the story is told that there are only two possible outcomes to the story – either Angela quits (which is absolutely unjust) or the other woman leaves. There is no real consideration of the option that something may be possible to change the situation with both of them still working together – the implication is that "one of us has to go".

Claire's story

Let's have a look at another example. This is a story told by Claire about a conflict she was experiencing with her flatmate.

> Emma and I were flatmates for two years. We got along so well. It was like living with a sister or my best friend. I never minded sharing my food with Emma, or my car for that matter. Emma always made up for it by making me dinner another night or giving me some petrol money if she had to drive the car a long way. Sometimes if we ran out of things, like sugar or something, I'd happily go and buy us some. I didn't mind because Emma would do the same on other occasions when she noticed we were getting low on something. I probably did replace things a bit more often than Emma, but, you know, I have a part-time job that pays well, and Emma was a student on a limited scholarship, so I didn't mind helping her out.

Anyway, when Emma moved out late last year, I advertised for a new flatmate. I didn't get too many people apply – it was the wrong time of year for people to be moving into a new place at the start of the summer holidays. I had to decide between Alison and Juan, and I picked Alison because I felt more comfortable sharing with a female.

Anyway, since she moved in things have been getting worse and worse. She is constantly using my food and she never asks. I walk into the kitchen and she's making a cup of tea, and she blatantly opens the fridge in front of me, gets out MY milk and pours it into her cup without batting an eyelid. It's outrageous, really. It's like she's daring me to challenge her.

And it's not just little things like a bit of milk for her tea. One night I got home from work and I was going to make a stir-fry. I had especially gone shopping for all the ingredients on the weekend and had exactly what I needed. Anyway, I started preparing the meal and I realised that my aubergine was missing: an essential ingredient in my stir-fry. And, I mean, who steals an aubergine???! It's not even a normal food item! So I couldn't make the stir-fry that I had planned so carefully. It was so annoying and I ended up just having a piece of toast and going to bed hungry.

It's got so bad now that every time I hear her in the kitchen I am convinced that she is stealing my food. I'm constantly on edge. If I see her in the lounge watching TV, I can't even bear to go and sit in there with her, and I just go to my room. I am like a prisoner in my own house. It has to stop. I have exams in a couple of weeks and I can't concentrate. I definitely can't study at home. It's just too stressful.

I want her to move out, but I can't even speak to her right now, I am so angry. I'm worried that she won't agree to go, and then what will I do? She signed a six-month lease and there are still three months to go. I'm completely trapped.

What do you think I should do? Is there a way you can make her move out?

Claire's story review

Reading Claire's story, you can probably already begin to recognise some of the similarities with the genre of melodrama. Claire doesn't like the uncertainty of the situation – she wants things to be sorted out, and fast! In particular, she wants things to return to the way they were before Alison moved in, when she had the perfect flatmate and was happy. There are two main characters in the story: Claire (the virtuous heroine) and Alison (the evil villain). Claire spends some time demonstrating what a good flatmate she is by describing her past relationship with Emma.

The story is sensationalised – Claire uses exaggerated language like "she is *constantly* using my food and she *never* asks"; she feels like "a prisoner" who is "completely trapped" and "constantly on edge". There is some over-dramatisation – not only does Alison use Claire's milk, but she steals her aubergines, not even a "normal food item"! She explains Alison's actions as morally wrong and intentional – "she *blatantly* opens the fridge in front of me", "without batting an eyelid"; it's like Alison is daring Claire to challenge her.

Though Claire describes Alison's actions, there is little discussion of her own actions. For example, she doesn't describe what she does when Alison uses her milk in front of her or when she finds her aubergine missing. She talks a lot about what she could not or cannot do: she couldn't make the stir-fry she was planning, she can't go into the lounge when Alison is there, she can't study at home. She can't even speak to Alison right now.

The story is overly simplified to emphasise Alison's bad actions. However, apart from the gaps around Claire's actions, there is probably some history and context that might shed some light on the situation. For example, what sort of discussions did they have when Alison moved in about food, sharing, etc.? Does Alison have any food of her own in the house? Has Claire ever used anything belonging to Alison? There is probably a lot more useful information available to Claire – not necessarily to prove who is right or wrong in the situation but rather to paint a more nuanced picture of what has led up to this situation.

Claire emphasises how much she is suffering as a result of Alison's actions. She is annoyed, she had to go to bed hungry, she is constantly on edge, she can't concentrate to study, she is stressed, she's angry, she's worried, and she doesn't know what to do. Objectively, it seems like a lot of suffering over some milk and an aubergine.

The story implies only two possible outcomes to this situation – Alison stays for the next three months and Claire suffers or Alison is somehow forced to move out.

Kevin's story

Here's a story told by Kevin about his workplace conflict.

> I've been working at this firm for years. I am well respected by my colleagues and my work is seen as excellent. My performance reviews are always positive. I applied for a position as team leader for this new project coming up, but to everyone's shock, I didn't get it. One of the guys from another department got appointed to the role. Nobody could believe it. I was the obvious candidate for the job. Anyway, this guy Bill arrives and pretty soon starts to mess everything up.
>
> Before he took over, we all got along just fine and did our work; everyone was happy and productive. Then he came along. He is one of those people who loves to put the cat among the pigeons. He goes out of his way to criticise others and he makes snide remarks all the time. He likes to set people up against each other – he just loves creating conflict!
>
> At first I tried to give him the benefit of the doubt, you know, thinking maybe he was just a bit insecure about coming into such an established team. But pretty soon I realised that he was just a jerk.
>
> He's now set out on a campaign to undermine me. Whenever I suggest anything, he just rolls his eyes and says, "Well, that won't work, obviously", and if I dare question any of his decisions he completely blows his top. He has even yelled at me in front of the whole team, shouting that I didn't have a clue what I was talking about. He accused me of not being a team player. It's outrageous. He is making my life a complete misery.
>
> I don't think I can work in the team anymore but there are no other vacancies in other areas of the firm. I can't afford to quit the job, I have a mortgage to pay. I'm completely stuck. I'm not sure how long I can take this psychological warfare. I'm starting to get sick, and I know it's because I'm so stressed. I'll probably end up with cancer or something because of this guy.
>
> My wife said I should speak to the manager about this, put in a grievance or something, but I don't want to look like I can't get along with my colleagues. I just can't speak to her about it.

Kevin's story review

Kevin sets the scene for the melodrama to start when he describes a workplace in which everyone gets along, he is respected, and his work is recognised as excellent. However, then the bad guy, Bill, comes along. He receives something he didn't deserve (the promotion) and, not only that, he took it away from Kevin, who did deserve it.

Kevin describes Bill as intentionally creating conflict and undermining Kevin. He provides a number of examples in which Bill interacts with him inappropriately in front of others and implies that all of their interactions are this way. Not only is Bill's behaviour inappropriate but what he says about Kevin challenges things that Kevin values about himself (that he knows what he's doing and that he's a team player who gets along with his colleagues).

When describing the events so far, Kevin focuses on Bill's behaviour (rolling his eyes, blowing his top, yelling at him in front of the team, questioning his ability) and how this makes Kevin suffer. Kevin does not provide any information on how he reacts when Bill says those things.

Kevin uses highly emotive language, such as "it's outrageous", "he's making my life a complete misery", "psychological warfare", and even suggests that he may end up with cancer because of Bill's behaviour.

Kevin also portrays himself as helpless in the situation. He's completely stuck. He can't speak to his manager about it. He can't quit and he can't stay.

Conclusion

As you read the three stories told by Angela, Claire, and Kevin, did you notice the similarities between them even though the characters and the context in which their conflicts occurred were different? Though each of their conflict stories are different, they are all told consistently with the melodramatic conflict narrative. They are stories about unfairness, suffering, and being stuck. They are stories about a "bad guy" who unfairly threatens what the storyteller values in themselves, deliberately in order to make the storyteller suffer. They are stories in which the "bad guy" has all the power and the storyteller is helpless and mute. The implied endings are that one of them (the storyteller or the bad guy) has to go and that the only fair outcome is for the bad guy to leave so that the storyteller can be put back in their rightful position. The basic plot structure is the same, and the character portrayals are based on stock types and behaviours. We will refer back to these three stories in later chapters to see how they developed during coaching.

4

MELODRAMATIC VICTIMS

In this chapter, we will consider the equivalent of the heroine role in the melodramatic conflict narrative. When people in conflict tell their story, they tell it from their own perspective as the main character in the story. Though they do not explicitly think of themselves as a heroine (especially if they identify as a man), they are likely to incorporate some attributes of the melodramatic heroine in the way they characterise their role in the story, including virtue, passivity, muteness, and suffering. For convenience and to acknowledge that this role can be played by people of different genders, when referring to this role in relation to conflict stories (rather than in classical melodrama) I will refer to this role as the "protagonist".

The protagonist role is a comforting one – we can reassure ourselves that we are innocent and virtuous and that we deserve to be rescued. However, there are some downsides to this role, particularly in the way in which it encourages us to ignore our contributions to the situation, to dwell on our suffering, and to remain passive and helpless.

DOI: 10.4324/9781003128038-4

The need to demonstrate virtue

When I meet clients who have come to me for coaching for the first time, they usually start off by telling me a bit about themselves. Partly, this is a way to build some rapport, to make a personal connection. It is also a way for them to test out how I respond to them – do I seem to be someone who can relate to them, who they can trust to support them with their conflict situation? At the same time, they also seem to intuitively feel like they need to show me that they are deserving of assistance.

Though I, as a conflict coach, do not require my clients to be perfectly innocent to utilise my services, there is a strong social expectation that to gain support as a victim, one must be deserving. In melodrama, because of the Manichean nature of the characters, virtue is an all or nothing concept. Any flaw in the protagonist's character brings her entire virtue into question and makes her undeserving of assistance. Accordingly, people in conflict will go to great lengths to demonstrate their virtue and also to divert attention from any areas in which they may have behaved less than perfectly.

In classical melodrama, the heroine's virtue was demonstrated by her purity, which in those times amounted to legitimacy of birth and virginity. In modern melodramatic conflict stories, virtue is defined according to what is valued by the protagonist and society in the context in which the conflict arises. In a workplace conflict virtue might be represented by a hard-working, honest, and friendly employee; in a family conflict virtue might be represented by a good parent who puts the interests of her children ahead of her own.

Demonstrating the protagonist's virtue is important in the melodramatic conflict narrative for a number of reasons: it portrays the protagonist as an innocent victim, which stands in stark contrast to the evilness of the villain; it emphasises the undeserved nature of the protagonist's suffering; it inspires sympathy and motivates others to help them; and it reinforces dream justice by making it clear that virtuous characters will always be rescued and rewarded for their suffering. Despite the fact that in real life virtue is never sufficient to preclude suffering, people in conflict still tend to present themselves as innocent victims in their conflict stories.

This emphasis on the protagonist's virtue is problematic for a number of reasons. Firstly, it assumes that pure virtue is possible, when in reality everyone is likely to be flawed in some respect – let's face it, nobody is perfect! Secondly, where virtue is a prerequisite for assistance, those in power from whom the protagonist seeks support are the arbiters of and define virtue. In other words, the person who is the equivalent of the father figure decides what is and what is not virtuous, and the protagonist must meet his criteria, irrespective of whether those criteria are consistent with the protagonist's true values.[1] Thirdly, the requirement of virtue implies that people who are less than perfect are not deserving of assistance or "dream justice".

Competing claims for virtue

As well as working as a conflict coach, I conduct mediations between people in conflict. In mediation cases I get to hear both sides of the story from the people involved. What I have noticed in this situation is the irony of the melodramatic conflict narrative, in that each person in the conflict casts themselves in the role of the protagonist and the other as villain, each maintaining that they are the innocent victim in the situation. Because there is an expectation that the other person is also going to identify as a victim and accuse the storyteller of being the villain, storytellers invest much energy into demonstrating their virtue and the other person's flaws.

Sally's story

Sally's story of conflict with her new supervisor Vivian provides a good example of how competing claims for virtue play out in modern conflicts. When I first met Sally, she came to see me about a conflict with her new supervisor, Vivian. She approached her company human resources department to make a complaint about her supervisor bullying her, and they referred her to me for conflict coaching so she could consider her options for managing the situation, instead of, or at least prior to, making the complaint official. I asked Sally to tell me a bit about what had been happening and this is how she started her story:

> I've been working at this company for five years now. During that time I have never had any problems with any other employees. I pretty much get along with everyone. I work hard; in fact, I'm often in the

office by 7.30 am and when there's an important project to be completed I am always happy to stay late. I like to socialise with my team
– I go to after-work drinks almost every Friday. We have a lot of fun.
My team is full of great people. I like to have fun at work, too – not too
much though. I'm not one of those people who has 20-minute coffee
breaks every hour and chats to people all day in the corridors. I do a
full day's work. But I'm also pretty easygoing. I like to check in with
people to see how they are going and to give them a hand if they are
snowed under.

From this description, Sally presents as the perfect employee with a com-
mendable work ethic. I'm starting to wonder how her supervisor could
possibly behave badly towards such a model staff member. I mean, what is
there not to like about Sally?

Already the melodramatic dichotomy is starting to be established
in Sally's story. The foundations for demonstrating that the supervisor's
actions are unjustified and even immoral have been laid. Also, I'm starting
to sympathise with Sally, hoping that I can help her find a way to get back
to being that fun-loving and hard-working employee again.

The funny thing is, had my client been Vivian instead of Sally, I'm sure
that she would have presented herself in a similarly virtuous light. Vivian
would probably have told me that she had come to see me because she had
been unfairly accused of bullying a staff member. She would likely have
told a story that started off something like this:

I've been working at this company for about six months now. I was
employed to take over managing the customer service team. When I
applied for the job, I was really keen to have this opportunity, and the
feedback from recruitment after my appointment was really encouraging. They said I was by far the best candidate for the role and they were
really impressed by my qualifications, experience, and references. I've
managed teams before, and I am good at getting dysfunctional teams
back on track. My team members respect and like me; they know I am
firm but fair and that my door is always open. I knew that this role was
going to be a particularly challenging one, but I felt really ready and
enthusiastic about it.

If I had been Vivian's coach, at this point I can imagine what I would have
been thinking: "Vivian seems to be a great supervisor, and other people

seem to think so, too. This staff member who has accused her of bullying must be a really difficult or overly sensitive person – Vivian doesn't seem like the bully type."

The important thing about acknowledging people's tendency to present themselves as virtuous in their conflict story is not to completely buy into their self-description, nor to treat it as deliberately fabricated. Rather, we need to accept the portrayal for what it is – a somewhat limited characterisation of the storyteller told for a particular purpose. What the client needs is acknowledgement, empathy, and reassurance that you are committed to supporting her in a nonjudgemental way. This provides a safe space for the client to later develop her own characterisation in ways that might be challenging and confronting for her.

The need to remain passive

As well as virtue, passivity is an essential attribute of the melodramatic heroine role. Cloke and Goldsmith (2000) describe this attribute of conflict stories as follows:

> In every conflict story we have heard, people position themselves as victims for one reason: to trade power for sympathy. Through their stories, they surrender their power in order to win a sympathetic response from their listener. They learn that the sympathy they receive increases in proportion to the other person's evil, which is measured partly by their own helplessness.
>
> (26)

In the melodramatic conflict narrative, the protagonist is passive in three respects: Firstly, they are passive in terms of the cause of the conflict – it is the villain whose actions give rise to the conflict. The protagonist is simply the passive victim of the villain's conduct. The second and third respects relate to the melodramatic "theme of failure" (Halliday, 1972, as cited in Jacobs, 1993, 121), in that the protagonist cannot resolve the situation in which they find themselves. They are passive in the sense of not being responsible for their continued suffering and passive in terms of the resolution of the story.

Passivity in relation to cause of the conflict

The need to present the conflict story in a way that establishes the protagonist as a passive victim means that they frequently ignore, downplay, or even actively hide their part in the conflict. Things are done *to* them rather than *by* them, and their stories tend to focus on the actions of the villain. In traditional melodrama, the story is first about the heroine's virtue, then the evil actions of the villain, then a request for dream justice. The actions of the villain are what are being judged. The heroine's actions are just not relevant in the melodramatic story. The only reason the heroine's actions would be overtly considered would be to call into question her virtue. If the heroine does nothing, then she cannot do anything to tarnish her virtue. Passivity is a strategy to maintain virtue.

In personal injury litigation, when someone sues for compensation for an injury caused by somebody else's negligence, even when that other person is found to have been clearly negligent, the compensation awarded may be reduced if the injured person is found to have contributed to the cause of the injury in some way (contributory negligence). In melodrama, however, the consequence of having contributed to the conflict arising is that the person loses entirely the right to dream justice. Melodrama is an all-or-nothing, win/lose game. There is no discounting of dream justice where the heroine has been less than completely virtuous. There is no room for compromise.

Bridget's story

Bridget's story provides a more dramatic example of a conflict client presenting as passive in relation to a conflict. Bridget came to see me about conflict she was having with an ex-boyfriend who worked at the same organisation. She explained that he was constantly harassing her, sending her nasty emails and text messages. She produced a bundle of pages on which she had printed out examples of some of the emails he had sent her. Their content was indeed unpleasant. She talked about the history of their relationship and breakup and what it had been like working with him after their relationship had ended. She described a "constant barrage" of horrible messages and said she was at a loss to explain why he persisted in sending them.

When I asked what she did when she received a message from him, she answered by describing how much they upset her. Her answer focused on the impact that these messages were having on her (her suffering) rather than her actions in response to receiving them. When I asked her to elaborate in relation to what she actually *did* after receiving a message, she admitted with some hesitation that sometimes she replied to the message. "Sometimes?" I asked her. "Well, nearly always. I mean, I can't just pretend they aren't arriving, can I?" she replied. I asked whether she could tell me about some of the replies she had sent. Reluctantly she opened up her laptop and showed me the long trail of email exchanges between them. Predictably, many of her replies were just as nasty as those he had sent to her, and it was by no means clear "who started it".

Sometimes the protagonist omits actions they have taken from their story because the protagonist feels that they are not particularly significant in the story. Other times their actions are not mentioned because admitting them calls into question their virtue. As Frank (2010) explains, people prefer to keep nonnarratable what they want to believe did not or does not happen. However, this avoidance of discussing one's own actions is frequently not a conscious decision. Usually, the client in conflict is not deliberately hiding information about their actions. In fact, when they are asked direct questions about their actions in a conflict situation, they are often quite surprised to realise that they have taken some!

Passivity in relation to suffering

The protagonist role also requires a passive response to suffering so that the protagonist is seen as pitiable. This is important so that the father figure develops the appropriate feeling of sympathy, including the motivation to take action to ease the heroine's suffering. The heroine's inability to ease her own suffering is required before the father figure can make a decision to assist her.

People in conflict often present as unable to minimise the impact the villain's actions are having on them, despite the fact that, objectively, there are sometimes things that they could do to help themselves. Again, this ignoring (perhaps even repressing) of harm minimisation strategies is usually not intentional. People in conflict are so captivated by the passive, suffering victim role that they no longer realise that there are things they can do to improve how the situation affects them.

George's story

George complained that his colleague Peter told their manager that George would not be able to join the team being put together for the next big project because it required some Saturday work and George had to coach his son's soccer team on Saturdays. George was indignant about this, because if he were offered a place on project, he said he would be able to find someone to take over as soccer coach for the period of the project work. George explained how worried he was about his prospects for promotion if he was not on this new project and how angry he was at Peter for interfering. However, when I asked George whether he had spoken to his manager to let him know that he was interested in working on the project and would be available on Saturdays if he was offered a place on the team, George's reply was a flat "I can't, he's too busy, and it's impossible to catch him for that kind of conversation right now". Objectively, it seemed that if George really wanted a place on the team, there was likely to be a way for him to get that message to the manager, even if it seemed difficult to arrange a meeting to discuss that at the time. However, what was interesting about the way George explained the situation was that getting his message to the manager was not presented as something that was difficult to organise – rather, it was presented as an impossibility.

Passivity in relation to resolution

The protagonist's passivity in relation to resolving the conflict is typical in the melodramatic conflict story. A common example of this is when clients express that they don't know something or they are lacking information that would be useful for them. When telling me their conflict story, clients often say things like, "I can't understand why she did that" or "I don't know what he was thinking". When I ask them what steps they have taken to try to find out why the other person behaved in this way or what the other person was thinking, they are often dumbfounded by the question. Not only have they typically done nothing to try to gather useful information but the possibility of doing so has not even occurred to them.

When I ask clients what they have tried to do to resolve the problem they are facing, a common response is "there's nothing I can do". They feel powerless to manage the situation and that they have no choice but to continue to suffer until someone rescues them. They frequently cannot see any possible actions they could take to improve the situation. This feeling of being "stuck" in the conflict is very common. The protagonist presents as helpless to do anything and as having no choice in the situation but to continue to suffer.

No choices

The fallacy of having no choices is a fundamental part of the melodramatic conflict narrative. The reality is, however, that there are always choices. At the most basic level, there are always two choices: to do something or to do nothing. The option of doing something comes with infinite variations – a person could do something now or do something later; could do it quickly or do it slowly; could do it with support or alone; etc. Protagonists in the melodramatic conflict narrative do not see these potential choices.

Why do protagonist deny choices exist? Firstly, *making choices requires active work*. We must identify different options, evaluate their potential risks and benefits, and decide between them. It can be easier to passively wait for someone else to make a choice than to put significant effort into doing it oneself. However, the longer we wait to make a choice, the harder it can be to make. When this becomes a pattern, we can develop "learned helplessness" (Seligman, 1972), which affects our future motivation to make choices. It is important to note, however, that deferring choice is a choice in itself. In the melodramatic conflict narrative, this is denied, and lack of choice is presented as something imposed on the protagonist from external (evil) forces.

Secondly, *there is considerable risk in making a choice*. What if we make the wrong one? Frequently, the status quo is not as risky – at least it is known. Anticipated regret can lead to paralysis (Schwartz, 2004). Schwartz also explains that we tend to have an *omission bias*, in that we downplay omissions (failures to act) when we evaluate the consequences of our decisions. In the short term we are more likely to regret actions that don't turn out well than to regret failures to take actions that would have turned out well.

Thirdly, if it doesn't work out, *we can blame somebody else*. When somebody else takes on the effort of making a choice for us, we can lay upon them the responsibility for any consequences of that choice. Recognising that choices are available also makes it clear that it is at least partially your responsibility for the situation being as it is, in that you have a chance to change it and are not taking it.

Fourthly, we may be *gaining something by not making a choice*. For example, we may see a certain small gain (avoiding interacting) as better than an uncertain larger gain (conflict resolution).

Fifthly, in the melodramatic conflict narrative, the protagonist is typically *waiting for the perfect choice* (dream justice), an often pointless quest. This tendency to think about the world as it *might be*, based on counterfactual thinking, tends to be triggered by something unpleasant giving rise to a negative emotion – such as being in a conflict situation. Schwartz (2004) describes this mindset of delaying action in anticipation of the perfect solution as having "the goal of maximizing" (78) and explains that it is a source of great dissatisfaction.

Choices in the melodramatic conflict narrative are presented as all-or-nothing, win/lose choices. Clients often present their choices as succumb to the villain's power and suffer or let the villain win by running away. For example, Angela sums up her story about conflict with her colleague by saying:

> ... the only solution I can think of is quit the job, and don't do something which is not making you happy anymore, but do I really have to quit this job for someone who is not worth my time?

This is typical melodramatic all-or-nothing thinking. Either her colleague goes or she goes – there is no room for consideration of something else, no awareness that there may be a way that they both could work together in the future.

The paradox of passivity and the denial of choice by the protagonist is that we hate the fact that we have no choice, and yet we are not prepared to recognise the choices we have made and could yet make.

Muteness

A specific aspect of passivity that is frequently found in melodramatic conflict stories is the protagonist's muteness when it comes to advocating for their own needs. Most experts in the field of conflict agree that much of the conflict we experience is based on lack of or miscommunication. When people in conflict communicate effectively and really understand each other's needs and concerns, they often find a way to resolve or at least manage the conflict more effectively. However, what is very common for many people in conflict is the feeling that they cannot talk with the other person. In a melodramatic conflict story, the protagonist is unable to talk to the villain or the powerful decision maker, because of either physical or socially imposed muteness. They are unable to share important information about their virtue, express their needs, or negotiate a resolution to their suffering.

Angela's story

Let's go back to Angela's story that we introduced in Chapter 3. Angela provided a good example of the concept of muteness when she described her interaction with her colleague about where she was going to sit. She explained that when Georgia made the comment about Angela wanting her desk and chair she wanted to "give it back to her" but in that moment she was "tongue-tied". Though in some respects, it would not have necessarily been the wisest choice for Angela to have "given it back to her" on her first day at work, Angela does not present her failure to do so as a choice. She doesn't say that she took into consideration social constraints on how you should talk to your colleagues and decided that she would be better not to say what she really wanted to reply to Georgia in that moment. Rather, she says that she *couldn't* say anything because she was tongue-tied. Similarly, Angela later said that:

> There's absolutely no way I can talk to her about it because she's just going to be like, ... "What, didn't they teach you at uni how to deal with all these things?"

The only reason Angela gives for her inability to talk with her colleague is that her colleague is likely to respond with her standard line about Angela's university education. There doesn't seem to be any logical connection between what she expects her colleague to say in reply and her expressed inability to talk with her about the situation. Angela does not recognise that she is making a choice not to talk with her colleague based on her expectations of how that conversation might go. However, objectively there may be a variety of options as to how she could approach her colleague about the situation and a range of things she could say or do if her colleague reacts as expected.

Suffering

In melodrama, it is imperative that the protagonist demonstrate suffering as a result of the villain's actions. The protagonist's suffering is important to stimulate pathos in the audience and motivate the audience to assist her. The more extreme the suffering, the more evil the villain's actions appear. The villain's intention goes without saying – if the impact of the villain's actions is suffering, then the villain must have intended to harm the protagonist in this way. There are no accidents in melodrama. Impact and intention are always aligned.

Exaggerated suffering

The protagonist's suffering is presented in an exaggerated and sensationalised manner. In classical melodrama the heroine is often cast out of her home, stripped of the rights of the virtuous, left poverty-stricken and starving, or imprisoned in a dark and cold dungeon. In modern-day melodramatic conflict stories, the protagonist's suffering is a contextually appropriate equivalent, often including psychological and physical consequences, a sense of being trapped, and potential professional or financial ruin. For example, in Angela's conflict story, she twice describes going to work as "a nightmare". In Kevin's conflict story, he describes how his colleague is making his life "a complete misery", how he is starting to get sick because he is so stressed, and that he will "probably end up with cancer or something" because of his colleague's behaviour. Claire is "constantly on edge", is "completely trapped", and feels like "a prisoner in [her] own home". She seems likely to fail her exams because of the constant stress.

Idealised past to highlight suffering

In order to establish the value of the preconflict state, the melodramatic conflict narrative begins with a portrayal of the protagonist in an idealised past. Ideally the protagonist is portrayed as having been physically well and emotionally happy, in addition to being able to fulfil their social roles. They are held out to have lived a "whole" life prior to the conflict. Their life is then transformed by the villain's actions into one typified by extreme suffering. The starker the contrast between the preconflict and the postconflict states, the more extreme the protagonist's suffering appears. A common example used to demonstrate contrast effect is the fact that a swimming pool will seem so much colder if you sit in the sauna for a while before getting into the pool. In the same way, the protagonist's suffering will seem so much more severe if the condition they were in before the villain's actions was seen as one of perfect happiness.

Thus, the conflict itself tends to be described in terms that emphasise the severity of the protagonist's suffering and its continuing nature and negative consequences, in contrast with the protagonist's preconflict well-being.

Mary's story

A modern-day example of this can be found in Mary's story. Mary sustained a back injury at work owing to her employer's negligence. She explains that as a result of the injury she can now no longer perform her work-related duties and also that her life outside of work has been significantly impacted. She describes how she can no longer perform simple household tasks like vacuuming the floor. To emphasise her suffering, she explains how important such tasks were to her prior to the injury. Mary describes the pride and joy she took in keeping her house clean and tidy and how she saw these tasks as an inherent part of her identity as a good wife and mother. She emphasises the fact that being unable to vacuum has made her feel like "less of a woman". Without necessarily denying Mary's sense of value in keeping her house clean, it seems likely that in the past there were times when she didn't enjoy vacuuming and when she would have been very glad to think it possible that she would never have to vacuum again. Had someone offered her a gift of a housekeeper, she probably would have been very grateful to be relieved of those duties. However, in the context of the conflict with her employer about her injury she presents the loss of her ability to vacuum as a cause of suffering.

Examples of idealising the past can be seen in some of the other conflict stories we have examined so far. Kevin presents his life at work, prior to his colleague getting promoted above him, as characterised by him being respected by his colleagues and being recognised as producing excellent work. He explains that before his colleague took over as team leader "we all got along just fine and did our work; everyone was happy and productive". Claire talks about living with her previous flatmate Emma as being like living with a sister or a best friend; they got along so well, shared everything, and had a relationship based on reciprocity.

Appropriate response to suffering

In the melodramatic conflict narrative, it is also important that the protagonist demonstrates an appropriate response to suffering. In both literature and life we see examples of people who are judged because they are not seen as suffering enough. In Camus's (1998) book L'etranger, Meursault is accused of having murdered his mother, because he did not grieve appropriately after her death. In Australia in 1980, mother Lindy Chamberlain claimed that a dingo had taken her missing baby from her tent. She was disbelieved and (ultimately found to be wrongly) convicted of the murder of her baby and reviled in the media because of her stoic demeanour in the weeks and months following her baby's disappearance.

Similarly, it is important that the protagonist not be seen to derive any pleasure or satisfaction from her conflict situation. There are problems if the protagonist appears not to suffer enough or seems happy with any changes to her life subsequent to the villain's actions. For example, it wouldn't be consistent with the melodramatic nature of the story if Mary admitted that she quite liked the fact that her husband was now required to contribute to the housework by doing the vacuuming instead of Mary. Any factors that moderate the extremeness of the protagonist's suffering must be downplayed. Any mention of improvements in the protagonist's condition must be brushed over or immediately followed with a negative aspect. For example, if Mary acknowledges having some benefit from her husband contributing more to the household chores subsequent to the accident, she is likely to follow this by pointing out that this is creating a strain on their relationship, because her husband does not see this as part of his accepted role in the marriage. Accordingly, Mary suffers as a result of any benefit she receives, effectively negating the benefit.

Conclusion

As you can see, the protagonist role in a melodramatic conflict story may be comforting in the short term, but it's not likely to be helpful in the long term. A person who expends considerable energy trying to appear to be perfectly virtuous, who denies any possible contribution to the situation they find themselves in, who remains passive and does nothing to help themselves, and who focuses on their suffering is not likely to develop constructive strategies or resilience. Worse still, these behaviours can become habits over time and have significant negative impacts on a person's general well-being into the future. The good news is that there is a way out of the melodramatic victim role, as we will explore in the second half of this book.

Note

1 An example of this might be an employer deciding whether or not an employee is suitable for a promotion. The employer values staff who go above and beyond what is required by their role and favours people who work very long hours for no additional pay. The employee is likely to promote their willingness to work in this way, even though they would personally much prefer to go home at 5 pm and spend time with their family, because they need their employer's support for their promotion application and they fear that they will not get it without presenting in this way.

REFERENCES

Camus, A. 1998. L'étranger [The stranger]. Paris: Gallimard.

Cloke, K. and Goldsmith, J. 2000. Resolving personal and organizational conflict: stories of transformation and forgiveness. San Francisco: Jossey Bass.

Frank, A. W. 2010. Letting stories breathe: a socio-narratology. Chicago: University of Chicago Press.

Jacobs, L. 1993. The women's picture and the poetics of melodrama. Camera Obscura 31: 120–147.

Schwartz, B. 2004. The paradox of choice: why more is less. Pymble, NSW, Australia: Harper Collins.

Seligman, M. E. 1972. Learned helplessness. Annual Review of Medicine 23: 407–412.

5

MELODRAMATIC VILLAINS

The melodramatic conflict narrative requires the identification of a specific character to blame for the protagonist's suffering. If the protagonist is completely innocent, then someone else must be guilty of causing their suffering. This is the role of the villain. As explained in Chapter 2, the villain is typically demonised and presented as only doing bad things. There is frequently a moral undertone to how people in conflict speak about the other person. The other person is not simply someone who behaves in a way that the protagonist finds difficult – rather, they are the enemy of everything that is right and good. They are portrayed as having deliberately caused the conflict with the intention of making the protagonist suffer and gaining something they don't deserve. Villains are active and powerful and embody the opposite of what the protagonist is and strives for. They want to destroy what the protagonist values most. They do this simply because they are a bad person. No other reasons are required. The strength of the characterisation of the "other" as villain is often an indicator of the level of escalation of the conflict.

DOI: 10.4324/9781003128038-5

In this chapter, we will consider in more detail some of the attributes of melodramatic villains and how they affect the conflict dynamics.

Depersonalised

The person with whom the protagonist is in conflict is presented as a depersonalised stereotype of a villain. A common foundation for this depersonalisation is to avoid referring to the other person by their name. People typically refer to others they are in conflict with by labels such as "a colleague of mine", "this guy in my class", or "my ex". As the story progresses, it's not unusual to see the villain referred to using more inflammatory terms such as "the bitch" or "that jerk". Recall Angela's story, in which she started out acknowledging her colleague's years of experience but soon after suggested that she was enjoying making Angela suffer and finally described Georgia as "not even worth my time".

Making the other person seem less human makes it easier for us to stereotype them as the villain and motivate others to support us against them. It also, however, makes it harder for us to interact with the other person or to be interested in trying to understand them.

Powerful

Villains are characterised as being powerful, both over the protagonist and also over others who might be able to help clarify the protagonist's virtue. Often the villain's power is directly related to their high levels of activity and their ability to communicate with others, both of which are not necessarily connected to any official position of power. Villains are portrayed as clever and persuasive; they can get others to listen to what they have to say. They have access to power, either their own or the power of others whom they can trick into supporting their evil cause. They frequently disguise their villainous nature, so others unwittingly support them.

Here's an example of Jeff, describing Gavin, his colleague and the villain in Jeff's conflict story:

> He's manipulative but he is very clever about it. He manages up very well, so our manager just doesn't see how much of a bully he is. Even though we are technically on the same level, he treats me like I'm his

subordinate, and there's nothing I can do about it because the boss just agrees with whatever he says.

Focus on actions, not intentions

The melodramatic conflict narrative ignores the villain's subjective characteristics and focuses on the villain's actual behaviour and its consequences (the protagonist's suffering). This lack of internal depth of characters and the emphasis on the "what" rather than the "why" are classic features of melodrama.

The villain's actions are presented as consistently negative and based on bad intentions. Angela, for example, presents all of her colleague's actions as negative – none are merely neutral, much less positive. They are all presented as deliberate acts to make Angela suffer, and although there is little objective evidence to support Angela's description of her colleague's intentions, Angela presents them as facts.

> If I go to her for help ... she just looks at me and says, "Don't they teach this at uni?" or, if I do something ... good, she just says, "Is this all they taught you at uni?" And everything has the word "university" in it, or my degrees ... she's trying to make me feel inferior to her. ... I think she's enjoying it, because every time she says these things to me she says it with a smirk.

Similarly, Claire implies that her flat mate Alison's behaviour is deliberate, describing it as "*blatant*" and explaining that it's "*like she's daring [Claire] to challenge her*".

In the same vein, Kevin describes his colleague:

> He is one of those people who loves to put the cat among the pigeons. He goes out of his way to criticise others and he makes snide remarks all the time. He likes to set people up against each other – he just loves creating conflict! ... He's now set out on a campaign to undermine me.

Even when the villain's actions could potentially appear to be reasonable, the protagonist distrusts the villain's motivations and usually presents them as based on dishonest reasons. For example, my client Katie described her colleague Anna as being selfish and universally disliked in her organisation. She explained that Anna "walked all over everyone in her quest for promotion" and that "she only cares about herself and her own glory". Confronted with evidence that Anna had invested quite a bit of time mentoring Sally, another less experienced staff member, Katie was dismissive: "She only does that because in the mentoring sessions Sally has to talk to her about what's going on in her team. Anna is just using Sally as her spy to find out information for her own purposes". Katie explained the fact that Sally didn't seem to agree with this by describing how Anna was very clever at hiding her motivations from Sally, and Sally was just unknowingly being manipulated by Anna.

This portrayal of the villain as intentionally evil is the fundamental attribution error in action. This error explains our tendency to link other people's actions to intentions, while explaining our own behaviour by situational factors (Ross, 1977). When the villain behaves badly or performs an action that has negative consequences for us, we believe that they are doing it intentionally. However, in contrast, when we do something bad or that has negative consequences for others, we explain it as an accident or beyond our control. We don't allow that kind of leeway towards villains in our conflict stories.

No opportunity for explanations or excuses

Where the audience is not shown any character depth, they have little choice but to base their assessments on assumptions about the character's personality, abilities, and morality. In the context of melodrama, it is unnecessary to ask the question "Why did the villain act in this way?" because once it is established that the villain has put the protagonist's virtue in peril (an inherently blameworthy act), the "why" is answered by the simple fact that the villain is a bad character.

When I ask clients why they think the other person is behaving in the way they describe, they often don't need to think about this for very long, and their answers are matter of fact:

- He's clearly trying to undermine me.
- She's threatened by me.
- He loves creating conflict.

- She's just trying to make my life a misery.
- He can't cope with the fact that I've moved on with my life.

When I ask clients to explain to me what makes them believe that is the villain's motivation, they usually provide examples of the impact the villain's behaviour has on them, rather than evidence of the villain's intention. In other words, they blur impact with intention (Stone et al., 1999). If the villain's actions have caused the protagonist to suffer, then the villain must have intended to make the protagonist suffer, and there is no need to ask why he might do that – it is because he is an evil person.

Villain wants something he doesn't deserve

In traditional melodrama, the villain's actions are typically presented as stemming from his greed, jealousy, or general frustration in his inability to obtain (or keep) something he desires but does not deserve. This is also reflected in the melodramatic conflict narrative. For example, workplace conflict sometimes arises when a person is promoted and their former peer is now their subordinate. Where the protagonist is the subordinate, they will often present the former colleague as someone who obtained the promotion by deceit and who doesn't really deserve the higher role. The person who was promoted is portrayed as now using that power to make the protagonist suffer (either for no good reason or to ensure that others do not realise that the protagonist should actually have been the one promoted, not the villain). The protagonist often presents the villain as having obtained a promotion that really should have gone to the protagonist. This story is common, even when it turns out that the protagonist did not even apply for the promotion!

In contrast, where the protagonist is the person who has been promoted, they often present their former colleague as someone who, despite not having deserved it, feels that they have been unfairly denied the promotion and who is now going out of their way to make the newly promoted person's life difficult because of unjustified jealousy.

Individualised blame

In the melodramatic conflict story, because the villain is active and powerful it is logical that they are to blame for whatever happens. When the protagonist of the story doesn't *do* anything, it is more difficult to hold them accountable for any actions, simply because they are inactive! The other person ends up cast as the sole villain, which exacerbates the antagonism between the parties, reinforcing the already problematic effects of the melodramatic conflict narrative.

Tran's story

Tran is a PhD student locked in a bitter conflict with her supervisor Bridget. Bridget has recently submitted an annual report to the Graduate Research School in which she says that Tran is not meeting the requirements of this stage of her candidature. Tran says that the reason she has not been able to meet these requirements is because Bridget has not provided her with adequate supervision, and Tran has filed a complaint about Bridget to the university complaints service. Tran recently applied for a teaching fellowship at another university. She was notified that her application was unsuccessful and she wasn't even offered an interview. Tran believes that Bridget somehow sabotaged her application, by contacting one of the selection committee members at the other university to disparage Tran. She has no evidence of this but nonetheless is convinced that Bridget is responsible for her failure to be offered an interview for the position. Though this belief is problematic because it has led to Tran feeling incredibly negative towards Bridget and bad-mouthing her to anyone who will listen, it has also distracted her from a path of action that might be helpful to her – she has not thought to ask the other university for feedback on her application and why she wasn't offered an interview.

The other problem with individualised blame is that broader, systemic factors that may have caused or contributed to the conflict are repressed (as discussed earlier in Chapter 2 under The Melodramatic Plot). A good example of this situation arose with my client Harry. He was in conflict with his colleague Steve about their work roster. Harry believed that Steve was manipulating the system to ensure that his work hours suited his social life and sporting commitments and that this resulted in Harry having to work many undesirable night and weekend shifts and spending less quality time with his family. After exploring the situation in more detail, it became apparent that the roster system was far from perfect and allowed for this kind of unfair outcome. A few simple changes to the roster policy and rostering process could have prevented this situation from occurring in the first place and would ensure a more equitable system for everyone in the workplace, not just Harry and Steve.

Negative anticipation

In melodrama, the protagonist approaches the villain with negative anticipation. It is expected that whatever the villain does is intended to harm the protagonist. This can become a self-fulfilling prophecy. The protagonist becomes hypervigilant in observing the villain's actions and in evaluating them (inevitably negatively). The person cast in the villain role usually notices the protagonist's behaviour and becomes irritated (perhaps feeling "micromanaged" or "stalked" by the protagonist). This can then lead to the person cast in the villain role either trying to avoid the protagonist (interpreted as evasiveness), confronting them (interpreted as aggression), or responding in kind (interpreted as further examples of bad behaviour proving the protagonist's first impression).

Zero-sum thinking

The protagonist also engages in zero-sum thinking (Rozycka-Tran et al., 2015), where the villain's gain is the protagonist's loss and vice versa. In other words, anything that benefits the villain is seen to harm the protagonist, even when it actually has no direct impact on the protagonist (in German, it is known as gluckschmerz – feeling unhappy about the good fortune of others). The same works in reverse: when the villain suffers some kind of harm, the protagonist feels like they have been rewarded in some way, even if they actually gain nothing substantive as a result (a kind of schadenfreude – pleasure from another person's misfortune).

For example, Joe has recently discovered that his nemesis at work, Bill, has been successful in his application for a promotion. Joe is furious about this and spends a large amount of time complaining about how Bill's promotion is undeserved, how there were much better candidates who were unsuccessful, how Joe deserved the promotion much more than Bill, and how Bill was going to be terrible in his new higher role. With further questioning, however, it became apparent that, firstly, Joe hadn't actually applied for a promotion in this round of applications and, secondly, in Bill's new role he wouldn't actually have much contact with Joe anymore, because he would be leading a different team in another section of the organisation.

No empathy

Finally, the protagonist refuses to feel any empathy towards the villain. The protagonist presents as having nothing in common with the villain and as certain that there is no information that could divert this enemy perception; human feelings and ethical criteria towards the enemy are seen as dangerous and ill-advised.

Here's a great example from a client of mine who had just found out that his work colleague's dog had been seriously injured.

> He was late to work again, apparently because his dog had been run over. Frankly, I'm not surprised. He never cared for that dog properly. I heard he frequently went away for weekends leaving the dog at home – he didn't even put the dog in a kennel, and the poor thing didn't get fed for two days – imagine the poor neighbours – I bet it barked and barked while he was away. He probably left the gate open this morning and that's how the dog got onto the road in the first place. Poor dog, it's probably better off dead than living with him.

You are with us or you are against us

Not only does the protagonist refuse to show any empathy towards the villain of the story but they also judge anyone who does so. Protagonists have an all-or-nothing mindset that translates into "you're with me or you're against me" in relation to the villain. Anyone who demonstrates empathy or any kind of support for the villain of the story is automatically categorised as one of the villain's "henchmen". This can make it very difficult for anyone to try to help the protagonist see the villain in any other light, because any attempt to balance the protagonist's perspective can result in the protagonist refusing to listen any further to that person.

Conclusion

The melodramatic conflict narrative assumes that all conflict can (and should) be preventable and that conflict only arises when the villain deliberately acts in a way that upsets the moral order. However, in my experience, there are very few people in the world who wake up in the morning and deliberately decide to create conflict. Rather, most people would prefer not to have conflict in their lives and try to avoid creating it where possible. Usually, people find themselves in conflict situations through a combination of systemic factors, less than perfect conflict management and communication skills, mistakes, and poor choices.

Identifying and vilifying a "villain" in our conflict story may make us feel righteous, but it does not help us to manage the conflict well. It prevents us from seeing others with a balanced perspective, it shuts us off from communicating with those with whom we often most need to communicate, and it narrows down our options for moving forward and makes our future entirely dependent on another person, rather than ourselves.

REFERENCES

Ross, L. 1977. The intuitive psychologist and his shortcomings: distortions in the attribution process. *Advances in Experimental Social Psychology* 10: 173–220.

Rozycka-Tran, J., Boski, P. and Wojciszke, B. 2015. Belief in a zero-sum game as a social axiom: a 37-nation study. *Journal of Cross-Cultural Psychology* 46(4): 525–548.

Stone, D., Patton, B. and Heen, S. 1999. *Difficult conversations: how to discuss what matters most.* New York: Penguin Books.

6

THE PROBLEM WITH MELODRAMATIC NARRATIVES

In this chapter, we will consider why the melodramatic conflict narrative is so problematic and how it prevents us from effectively managing conflict. The melodramatic conflict narrative is pervasive and compelling because it provides us with comfort and certainty in times of confusion, it rallies sympathy and support, and it can make us feel secure in our moral righteousness. On closer analysis, however, it is fraught with danger. It narrows our thinking about conflict in general, it limits our opportunities for managing our specific conflict effectively, and it frequently leads us to frustration by holding up the false hope of a perfect outcome. Most important, it prevents us from learning and growing through our conflicts.

The melodramatic conflict narrative narrows our thinking about conflict

The melodramatic conflict narrative provides a framework into which we fit our individual conflict stories and, in doing so, it limits our thinking

DOI: 10.4324/9781003128038-6

about conflict in general, not just our own particular conflict situation. In other words, the melodramatic conflict narrative gives conflict a bad name! It teaches us that conflict is a bad thing. It portrays conflict as something that is caused by immoral people for evil purposes. It tells us that resolving conflict is an adversarial process between individuals, a fight between good and evil. None of these things are true; the reality of conflict is much more complex, and there are significant risks in believing them.

Teaches us that conflict is a bad thing

In the melodramatic conflict narrative, conflict is portrayed as something that, in a perfect world, should not exist. Conflict is something that should be avoided, corrected, and erased. The melodramatic conflict narrative allows us to act on the hopeful theory that all conflict can and should be resolved and that all suffering can and should be eliminated.

Accordingly, the benefits of conflict as an opportunity for increased understanding, development, and growth are denied. This happens because in melodrama, the resolution of any conflict results in the restoration of the status quo. The melodramatic conflict narrative prevents any possible criticisms of the status quo – there is an unspoken assumption that things should be the way they were before the villain's actions. This also denies any possibility for improving on the past. It ignores the potential benefits that conflict can offer us.

Teaches us that conflict is about individualised blame

In the melodramatic conflict narrative, conflict is caused by a morally reprehensible individual, the villain. We do not need to question why that individual acts in such a way – this goes without saying because of his evil nature. This personification of moral evil simplifies the often complex question of responsibility.

The melodramatic conflict narrative precludes any consideration of history or context that may have created the conditions in which the conflict could arise. With any given conflict, there will usually be a combination of factors incorporating human action, the conditions that made the conflict possible, and other factors that contributed to the conflict. However, the melodramatic conflict narrative converts a complex chain of conditions and events into a compact monocausal account focussing on the action of the villain.

Instead of uncovering the systematic origins of conflict, the melodramatic conflict narrative not only distorts conflict as having a single cause but also paints it melodramatically by finding a histrionically reprehensible flaw on the part of some single individual. Systemic factors are not just ignored, they are repressed. The melodramatic conflict narrative provides a certain amount of comfort to those who are suffering, without addressing some of the underlying causes of that suffering. As Heilman (1968) explains, "All resources are directed against the enemy ... hence a society can turn its energies of mind and passion away from examining itself" (105). The audience can enjoy the seductive pleasures of melodramatic wholeness without considering the contributions of and effects on those outside the limited melodramatic conflict narrative.

Teaches us that conflict is adversarial in nature

The melodramatic conflict narrative pits two individuals against one another: the protagonist versus the villain. Conflict is presented as Manichean in nature, a battle between good and evil, and it is a win/lose game. There is no room for compromise, and certainly no possibility of collaboration. Virtuous protagonists do not sit down and have conversations with villains, both because it this would be morally inappropriate (nice girls do not converse with bad guys) and because in the melodramatic conflict narrative the protagonist is effectively mute, which prevents her from entering into such a discussion at all.

The melodramatic conflict narrative is based on competition between protagonist and villain and also between their respective versions of events. The "villain" in one person's story is the "protagonist" in the other person's own story. To adapt Frank's (2010) words, the dilemma of the melodramatic conflict narrative is that people are caught up in their own melodramatic conflict story while living with people caught up in their own melodramatic conflict story. The telling of a melodramatic conflict story invites one in response – the "I'm the real victim here" reply.

The melodramatic conflict narrative restricts our opportunities for managing conflict effectively (now and in the future)

People whose conflict stories are constrained by the melodramatic conflict narrative are likely to be less able to manage or resolve their conflict effectively. This is because the narrative limits their access to useful information, encourages them to ignore their own contributions to the conflict, and incentivises victimhood and suffering.

Limits our access to useful information

Melodramatic conflict narratives, in their simplicity, divert our attention from information that might be useful to us in managing the conflict more constructively. When we have a narrow set of facts, we have an incomplete understanding of what is actually going on and also believe that we have more limited options than are available to us. Simplicity provides coherency, but conflict is often multifaceted and complex. When we make choices based on an oversimplified version of events, they are unlikely to be the best choices. They are not well-informed. There is likely to be other information that would assist us to better identify, evaluate, and prepare for our future choices, if we explore more deeply than the melodramatic conflict narrative allows.

The melodramatic conflict narrative focuses on actions by the villain and suffering of the protagonist. It excludes information about history, context, what happened in between the main actions by the villain, any actions taken by the protagonist, other characters' actions and perspectives, etc. This missing information could provide us with a more nuanced understanding of how the conflict came about and how it could be managed more effectively.

We are encouraged to ignore our own contributions

When conflict is seen as morally wrong and characters are consistently either good or evil, then only evil characters can create conflict. We therefore cannot admit any contribution to conflict without being characterised as evil. Though the melodramatic conflict narrative could have a positive role to play in educating us about how to be virtuous, the problem with the melodramatic conflict narrative's presentation of morality is that it encourages us to see only good in ourselves and only evil in others. When we focus on the actions of others and blame their actions for the conflict, we can avoid paying attention to our own contributions. The melodramatic conflict narrative focuses our attention on action outside the human character, so we miss the inner action of sentience and responsibility.

Frank (2010) says that as the virtuous storyteller, we prefer to keep non-narratable what we want to believe did not happen. We may not deliberately omit or lie about our own actions and contributions, however: "We see in the past only what is important for the present, important for the instant in which we remember our past" (cited in Frank, 2010, 1861; he notes that this was credited to V. N. Volosinov but probably should be attributed to Bakhtin). In the melodramatic conflict narrative, what is important for the protagonist is information about her virtue and undeserved suffering. Frank (2010) describes these kinds of stories as "authentic fabrications" (1980). In Frank's words, stories often reflect more the protagonist's desire for what might have happened than commitment to an accurate description of what did happen We all wish that we could have been totally virtuous, despite the reality that this is rarely the case.

Incentivises victimhood, passivity, and suffering

The melodramatic conflict narrative actively discourages a proactive approach to conflict management. The appropriate thing to do is to remain passive and wait for rescue. Playing the passive protagonist role can have a kind of self-fulfilling quality by threatening the sense of control that allows a person to cope with conflict experiences. This limits the scope for the person to resolve some aspects of his or her own suffering by focusing on the judge as the dispenser of dream justice, rather than the protagonist having any independent control of his or her own destiny. The protagonist stagnates while waiting for dream justice. They are encouraged by the promise that suffering is necessary by offering future justice, which fosters an attitude of resignation, robbing them of energy needed to fight present injustices. It encourages passivity as the appropriate response to suffering. The psychological temptations of victim status tend to result in a loss of individual power by discouraging people who are categorised as victims from developing their own strengths or working to resist the limitations they encounter (Minow, 1993).

Fitting the protagonist role in the melodramatic conflict narrative can lead people towards a situation of learned helplessness. Learned helplessness occurs when "a person ... displays inappropriate passivity: failing through lack of mental or behavioural action to meet the demands of a situation where effective coping is possible" (Peterson and Bossio, 1989, 240). Learned helplessness is often encouraged and developed in situations where the person is "rewarded for passivity and/or punished for activity" (Peterson and Bossio, 1989, 240). The protagonist role, characterised by passivity and dependence on others, seems an ideal foundation for the development of learned helplessness. The melodramatic conflict narrative provides emotional compensations (and even rewards or enticements) for helplessness. The melodramatic protagonist is "saved the troublesome pains of responsibility for evil, of choice among unclear options, ... [and can easily] yield to the lure of passivity" (Heilman, 1968, 86).

Claiming remedies or entitlements on the basis of victim status gives individuals a stake in their victimisation (Taylor, 1991, as cited in Minow, 1993). The fact that the protagonist is rewarded by complying with the victim role places extra pressure on them to redefine themselves and their relationships in accordance with that role. The "language of victimisation invites people to treat victimhood as the primary source of identity" (Minow, 1993, 1433). This is especially problematic when these characteristics start to become a part of the personal narrative. As Carr (1985) points out, when people are explaining themselves to others they are "often trying to convince [themselves] as well" (117). Presenting oneself in accordance with this predefined role can change the future development of one's life narrative.

Concepts of self and identity are formed in the personal narratives people use to give meaning and completeness to their lives. Life narratives are constantly developed and revised as new events occur. In this way, one's concept of self is not static, and life narratives develop from both the past and expectations for the future (Polkinghorne, 1988). When social settings provide stock roles to guide behaviour (such as the protagonist role in the melodramatic conflict narrative) and reward those who comply, people tend to adopt those roles, even when they may appear to be inconsistent with an individual's lived experience. This effect is magnified when the story is required to be retold publicly, irrevocably, consistently, and under cross-examination, as happens in conflict.

In some ways, the helpless victim identity becomes a self-fulfilling prophecy. Because the protagonist in the melodramatic conflict narrative is discouraged from taking steps to manage the situation themselves or to alleviate their suffering, they also lose the opportunity to learn and develop the skills to do so. This can result in the person experiencing the same kinds of conflicts in their lives over and over, because each time they are faced with the same challenge they default to helplessness. They are not encouraged or supported to develop the strengths required to manage conflict now or in the future. Many conflict support professionals are not trained to deal with (and are probably unaware of) the fact that their clients are reconfiguring their identity during the conflict management and resolution process. When these become deeply ingrained life patterns, a more therapeutic intervention may be necessary.

The failure of dream justice leaves us disillusioned

The melodramatic conflict narrative suggests that as long as the protagonist remains virtuous and does not do anything to upset the moral order, eventually everything will be okay. Then, after all that waiting, we are inevitably disappointed. Either the dream justice that we have been waiting for never arrives or we do receive it but it does not live up to our expectations. We rarely feel as though the conflict never happened, the status quo is not fully restored, and at some level our suffering remains. The promised catharsis never happens.

Even when "dream justice" is apparently achieved, the melodramatic conflict narrative cannot actually restore the protagonist to his or her pre-conflict condition, and rarely is the protagonist's suffering totally alleviated. After conflict, things never go back to "the way they were before". There has been water under the bridge, and people have had experiences and witnessed interactions that will remain in their memories and potentially affect their future feelings and actions. The protagonist's supporters' congratulations, society's washing its hands of any further responsibility for their suffering, their sudden isolation after the withdrawal of support from others frequently leave "victorious" protagonists feeling less than the recipient of "dream justice".

This experience, however, does not necessarily act as a catalyst for the protagonist learning and developing a balanced view of the world (in which good things do not *always* happen to good people and bad guys do not *always* receive their comeuppance and in which life is sometimes not fair). Rather, the protagonist is likely to replace their prior basic assumptions about life and their role in it with one based on new assumptions such as "the malevolence of the world and people, the meaninglessness and randomness of the world, and the unworthiness of the self" (Janoff-Bulman and Thomas, 1989, 225). This can give rise to a negative redefinition of identity and detrimental effects on the healing process. People escape from being victimised by the villain in the melodramatic conflict narrative only to find themselves a victim of the world and its unjustness.

The melodramatic conflict narrative prevents us from learning and growing

Most important, experiencing conflict through the melodramatic conflict narrative prevents us from learning and growing through our experiences of conflict. When we are encouraged to think about conflict in a superficial way and to focus on the actions of others rather than our own and the promised resolution is the restoration of the status quo rather than an improvement, learning and growth are impossible. In the melodramatic conflict narrative, there is nothing new to be learned, and the story ends where it began; success is moving backwards, not forwards, and there is no growth or development in either the characters or the society in which they live.

Conclusion

Despite the problematic consequences of adopting the melodramatic conflict narrative as a framework for understanding one's own conflict, it is surprisingly common and challenging to shift. In the following chapters we will consider what makes a more constructive and realistic conflict story and how to facilitate a shift from melodrama towards that more helpful story framework.

REFERENCES

Carr, D. 1985. Life and the narrator's art. In Silverman, H. J. and Idhe, D. (Eds.), *Hermeneutics and deconstruction*, pp. 108–121. Albany, NY: SUNY Press.

Frank, A. W. 2010. *Letting stories breathe: a socio-narratology*. Chicago: University of Chicago Press.

Heilman, R. B. 1968. *Tragedy and melodrama: versions of experience*. Seattle: University of Washington Press.

Janoff-Bulman, R. and Thomas, C. E. 1989. Self-defeating responses following victimization. In Curtis, R. C. (Ed.), *Self-defeating behaviors: experimental research, clinical impressions, and practical implications*, pp. 215–234. New York: Plenum Press.

Minow, M. 1993. Surviving victim talk. *UCLA Law Review* 40: 1411–1445.

Peterson, C. and Bossio, L. M. 1989. Learned helplessness. In Curtis, R. C. (Ed.), *Self-defeating behaviors: experimental research, clinical impressions, and practical implications*, pp. 235, 240. New York: Plenum Press.

Polkinghorne, D. E. 1988. *Narrative knowing and the human sciences*. Albany, NY: SUNY Press.

7

TRAGEDY

THE ALTERNATIVE CONFLICT STORY

Given that I have so far argued that the genre of melodrama provides a dysfunctional framework for conflict stories, the logical question to ask is what is a better genre to support a more functional conflict story? The answer appears counterintuitive, but my research has revealed that the genre of tragedy is a much more constructive genre of conflict story, resulting in the main character experiencing learning and growth and developing conflict resilience (if not always a happy ending). In this chapter we will examine what makes tragedy a more constructive genre for conflict stories and contrast the tragic hero with that of the melodramatic protagonist.

Defining tragedy

In everyday conversation, the term "tragedy" is frequently used loosely to refer simply to the undesirable consequences of an event (e.g., someone young died in a car accident, which was a tragedy). There is a common

DOI: 10.4324/9781003128038-7

misperception of tragedy that it is allied to pessimism. However, tragedy as a genre incorporates much more than a story with an unhappy ending.

The search for an acceptable or universal definition of tragedy has been, in the words of Stephen Booth (1983), "the most persistent and widespread of all nonreligious quests for definition" (81). However, the generally accepted attributes of the tragic genre include complex characters and plot; a sense of uncertainty; imperfect, divided characters; evocation of the "tragic qualm" when the audience's idealistic views about fairness and justice are shown to be false; a main character with a "fatal flaw" whose actions contribute to a reversal in his situation (usually, but not completely, to his detriment); a recognition that things are not as they seemed; some kind of growth or learning through suffering; and the audience's emotions of pity and fear. The story centres around the actions and dilemmas of one main character, the tragic hero, and his individual struggle to make sense of the world. Tragedy involves some kind of positive re-evaluation of the experience, frequently including learning some important lesson – about oneself, about others, or about what's really important in life.

Let's consider two examples of tragic stories, one historical and one modern, to set the scene for our exploration of tragedy as a genre. The play Macbeth, by William Shakespeare, is commonly categorised as a tragedy. The story is about Scottish general Macbeth, whose attempts to win and keep the throne end up leading to his downfall. The story begins when Macbeth is told by three witches that he will become King of Scotland. His friend Banquo, however, is told that his descendants will inherit the throne. King Duncan is currently on the throne. Macbeth's desire and impatience to be king leads to him deciding to kill the king. He does so but regrets it immediately. Macbeth does become the new king as prophesised. However, he is plagued by insecurity and his paranoia leads him to kill Banquo, in an attempt to prevent Banquo's descendants taking the throne from him. However, Banquo's son escapes. Macbeth's wife, plagued by guilt, commits suicide, leaving Macbeth alone in his fight to keep his throne. A civil war erupts in an attempt to overthrow him. Too late, Macbeth realises he is doomed; he surrenders and is killed.

A more modern example can be found in Game of Thrones, and specifically in the character of Jaime Lannister. What I particularly like about this example is that the series begins as a stereotypical melodrama, with the good guys (the

Starks) and the bad guys (the Lannisters) behaving consistently with their virtuous or evil nature. However, as the story progresses, things become very complicated, characters behave inconsistently and are internally divided, and it is not at all clear who is right and who is wrong. Jaime Lannister is a terrific example of a tragic hero. He is a very complex character. On the one hand, he is a rich, violent, and smug son of an influential father, involved in an incestuous relationship with his sister Cercei. He engages in a great deal of bad behaviour (including pushing ten-year-old Bran Stark out of the window of a high tower after Bran sees him embracing Cercei in a distinctly non-brotherly manner). However, he also performs despicable acts for virtuous reasons (e.g., he killed his own King, whom he swore to protect, to save his city's innocent inhabitants from being slaughtered) and he performs good acts at unexpected moments (e.g., when he shows a great deal of kindness to Brienne, the woman knight, and when he continues to protect his brother Tyrion even after Tyrion murders their father). Throughout the series, as tragic heroes do, Jaime Lannister does a lot of soul searching. He sums up the complexity, uncertainty, and inconsistency of his world as a knight when he says, "So many vows. They make you swear and swear. Defend the king, obey the king, obey your father, protect the innocent, defend the weak. But what if your father despises the king? What if the king massacres the inno-cent?" His "fatal flaw" is his incestuous love for his sister, which in the end leads to his death with her in the Red Keep.

Complexity and uncertainty

One of the defining features of the tragic genre is that its characters and its plot are both complex and uncertain. Nothing is simple, nothing is as it seems, and the tragic hero struggles to make sense of a chaotic world. In tragedy, the hero and the audience are required to question everything that they took for granted and are not left with any clear-cut answers. Where melodrama panders to our desire for the comfort of certainty, trag-edy exposes us to the paradoxes of reality.

The tragic qualm

In addition to disassembling our characterisation of people as either good or bad, tragedy causes us to challenge our idealistic expectations about dream justice. Unlike melodrama, which provides an explicit demonstration and reinforcement of the moral order, tragedy provides a moral *exploration* (Brereton, 1968). In tragedy there is no clear right and wrong. Tragedy causes us to question the notion of a universal principle of fairness, justice, or equity. Tragedy reveals to us the fallacy in our common assumption that something like God, nature, or the moral order will ensure that justice will prevail. This is known as the "tragic qualm". Frye (1922) explains the tragic qualm as that "feeling of insecurity and confusion, as if it were a sort of moral dizziness and nausea, due to the vivid realisation ... of a suspicion which is always lurking uncomfortably near the threshold of consciousness, that the world is somehow out of plumb" (146–147). This feeling was certainly evoked in the *Game of Thrones* audience when the "good guys" kept getting unjustly killed and the bad guys started attracting our sympathy!

Imperfect and divided characters

One of the key characteristics of the tragic form is "dividedness" (Heilman, 1968). Unlike melodrama's monopathic characters, in tragedy they are internally divided, giving rise to contradictions and inconsistencies. Characters in tragedy are neither good nor bad. They are good people who are not perfect and sometimes make mistakes and bad choices. They are good people who can sometimes have evil desires and perform terrible deeds. Tragedy assumes that there is the possibility for good and evil in all of us.

Characters in tragedy face the challenge of navigating choices in a world of different and perhaps irreconcilable needs and ideals. Sometimes these different imperatives are internal (for example, tension between two different values that cannot both be enacted in the situation) or external (for example, tension between two individuals with different needs and opinions about what should happen). Heilman (1968) points out that tragedy portrays the dividedness of life and thus encompasses life in its wholeness.

The tragic hero

Traditional tragic heroes were usually men, because they needed to have the stereotypical masculine attributes of being active and independent, and have the capacity to make choices about their own future.[1] In more modern tragedies, tragic heroes are not as limited by gender stereotypes.

Some authors suggest that the tragic hero (illustrated in Figure 7.1) should be a person who is highly renowned and prosperous, in contrast to the protagonist in comedy, who should be a person seen as somehow lower in status that the audience. However, it seems that the status of the protagonist vis-à-vis the audience is not particularly important, as long as the audience can relate to the hero as somehow like them. They must be "one of us", not necessarily virtuous or necessarily free from profound guilt but someone who reminds us strongly of our own humanity (Leech, 1969). This is important because tragedy should evoke the emotions of pity and fear in the audience: pity because the hero's misfortune is seen

Figure 7.1 The tragic hero

as unmerited and fear because we recognise that the hero is a person like ourselves and that we too could suffer in the way they do.

Though at one level the audience in tragedy pities the tragic hero because he does not deserve his fate, we cannot be outraged that some evil character has unfairly caused him to suffer. Neither can we think that the hero "had it coming" like we may feel in melodrama when the villain receives his comeuppance, because we understand that the tragic hero is basically a good person doing the best he can in difficult circumstances. At the same time, however, we are forced to acknowledge the uncomfortable truth that the tragic hero was partially the author of his own destiny. In some sense, the tragic hero's poor choices have led to the outcome being inevitable. And yet, we pity him because we recognise that his failings are things that we ourselves may also have, and we fear because we understand that his tragic fall could be our own.

Hamartia: tragic flaw

The tragic hero is not perfect (unlike the melodramatic protagonist). He has some kind of flaw, which may be a moral fault or a simple error of judgement. In theatrical tragedy, the tragic hero's flaw is often extreme for dramatic effect (e.g., Macbeth's ego and greed; Jaime Lannister's incestuous relationship with his sister and his willingness to severely injure a child to protect this secret). However, in modern tragedy, the hero's flaw may be rashness, laziness, or lack of attention. It is something less than a crime; something that does not make the tragic hero an evil character. It is the kind of flaw we can recognise in ourselves.

Individual struggle

Tragedy is a story about the struggle of an individual. However, unlike melodrama, the struggle is not against some easily identified external villain. Rather, the tragic hero is engaged in a struggle against something representing the human condition. Miller (1949) describes tragedy as a struggle of an individual to gain what the individual sees as their rightful position in society. This place may appear to be withheld by a powerful other, social structures, or simply fate. Tragedy explores the various kinds of power that influence human existence.

Mandel (1961) explains that the most striking characteristic of the tragic hero is that he possesses a purpose – a drive or an ideal that insists on being gratified. The plot follows the tragic hero as he struggles to understand himself and his place in the world and as he refuses to submit to the way things appear to be. Williams (1966) defines tragedy as the tension between belief and experience. In other words, the tragic hero believes that things should be a certain way, but his experience presents a different version of reality. The tragedy arises when the hero understands that, despite his struggle, reality does not meet his expectations.

Active

The tragic hero is an active character. He actively seeks to understand the situation in which he has found himself and he actively tries to make the appropriate choices to move forward. Miller (1978) suggests that this activeness can itself be the hero's fatal flaw – "his inherent unwillingness to remain passive in the face of what he conceives to be a challenge to his dignity, his image of his rightful status" (8). He explains that the tragic flaw is not necessarily a weakness. Only those who accept their fate without retaliation are "flawless", but with this flawlessness comes a passivity and idealism that is in itself problematic, because it requires dependency on others. The reality of tragedy is that the hero has nobody to depend on. Nobody is going to come and rescue him. The tragic hero is essentially alone in the struggle and has to examine the situation and make difficult choices for himself.

Choice

In tragedy, the hero must recognise and make choices. Much of his internal dividedness – his challenge – comes from having to choose between different courses of action. Often, his flaw leads him to make the incorrect choice. However, the fact that he does actually make a choice is a sign of his strength. A character who is unable to make choices, like the melodramatic heroine, is too weak to become a tragic figure and is resigned to her fate. The tragic hero at least has the strength and consciousness to try, despite facing the risk of failure.

Anagnorisis: recognition

In the tragic plot there is a moment of recognition (anagnorisis), when the tragic hero realises the consequences of his choices and comes to understand his place in the scheme of things. He recognises, more particularly, the life he has created for himself, with an implicit comparison with the uncreated potential life he has forsaken (Frye, 1922).

This recognition is often described as the "moment of truth" in which the tragic hero moves from ignorance to knowledge. The tragic hero may see through some disguise or mistaken identity (e.g., when Oedipus recognises that he has killed his own father and married his mother) or discover some element in his environment (e.g., when Willy in *Death of a Salesman* realises the inherent falsity of the promises of the capitalistic, competitive system) or his own soul (e.g., when Hamlet realises that he has delayed out of cowardice) of which he has not been aware or which he has not taken sufficiently into account. This recognition comes with an instant and profound emotional reaction, and the hero's direction in the play is completely altered.

Peripeteia: reversal

Tragedy entails a reversal in the hero's situation (peripeteia) – a fall resulting in suffering, some disaster, or misfortune. This fall is ironic, in the sense that a course of action is undertaken that has the opposite consequences to those intended – success is expected but disaster results.[2] The tragic hero must somehow play a part in his own downfall – although it may be a very small action that sets of a train of events in motion that lead to disaster (Leech, 1969). In modern tragedy, the ending need not be complete disaster or the hero's downfall. It may simply entail a recognition that the hero has, to some extent, contributed to his own fate and that different choices along the way may have led to a better outcome.

Paradoxical union of victory and defeat

In tragedy, there is no idealistic happy ending; rather, the story ends in the "paradoxical union" of victory and defeat (Heilman, 1968). Rather than affirming the social order, tragedy "countenances its contradictions and explores the possibility that conflicts may be neither resolved nor mediated" (Aristodemou, 2000, 32). Whereas melodrama insists on total victory or defeat, tragedy "defines life as the paradoxical union of the two" (Heilman, 1968, 154). Tragic narratives "avoid easy classifications and facile resolutions" and go instead "(as Nietzsche would hope), beyond good and evil" (Aristodemou, 2000, 65). The tragic hero is never simply a loser in a social conflict nor a simple victor over evil. To put it simply, it's complicated!

Acceptance and growth

Tragedy deals with the hero's efforts to escape his destiny, and its conclusion is his reunion with destiny (Heilman, 1968). However, tragedy does involve the suffering person finding a mode of recovery by accepting and growing through suffering. In the tragic view of reality, the hero finds some inner strength that enables him to learn and grow, irrespective of the outcome of the story. Even when the tragic story ends badly, something vital is saved (Heilman, 1968).

When the tragic hero realises his flaw, he takes some responsibility for it ("Yes, I can see that it was my fault. I ought to have been more careful.") Despite the terrible consequences of his action, this self-discovery leads to some change for the better. The hero, in his new wisdom, becomes more admired by the audience at the end of the play – he gains "tragic stature". He does what he can to rectify his error at the end, and even though it may be too late to avert the crisis, there is still some greatness in his effort to resist, a triumph of the human spirit in his suffering.

Self-reflection

In melodrama, the heroine is trying to tell her story of virtue and suffering to the father figure, whom she needs to rescue her. In tragedy, the hero is telling his story of confusion and fallibility to himself. Heroes are engaging in a process of self-reflection, trying to make sense of the chaos and contradictions around them. This focus on self-reflection is demonstrated in Miller's (1978) definition of tragedy as "the consequence of man's total compulsion to evaluate himself justly" (9). It is tragedy because we inevitably find ourselves falling short of the ideal – we discover our "tragic flaw".

This process of self-reflection leads to learning and growth, if not a stereotypical happy ending.

Moving forwards, not backwards

Heilman (1968) suggests that a sound concept of tragedy may influence social well-being. This is nicely illustrated by the experience of Sam Cawthorn, a young Australian man now in his early 30s. When he was 26 years of age he was in a shocking head-on car accident in Tasmania, Australia. After being declared clinically dead, he was revived, and he survived, albeit with horrific injuries. Though he still has significant physical challenges as an ongoing legacy of his injuries, he describes himself as emotionally, mentally, and spiritually richer. His book, *Bounce Forwards: How to Transform Crisis into Success* (Cawthorn, 2013) is an exemplar of the tragic hero who grows from a crisis and does more than just restore himself to the precrisis status quo. Cawthorn explains in a media interview (*The Age*, 8 August 2013):

> *People always say we need to bounce back from natural disasters, from financial crises, we all use that terminology. I have a problem with that because it means when we hit a crisis, we're focused on bouncing back to that place before the crisis hit. Looking at my own life, my entire rehab team was focused on getting me back to that same job, that same environment. But something had changed in me, not only physically but emotionally as well. So I was not focused on going back to my previous life, I was focused on going forward to what I can become.*

Another example can be found in the varying responses to COVID-19. Some people are talking about getting through it and everything going back to the way it was before (melodrama) and others are talking about how the world will never be the same again and learning from our suffering through the pandemic to improve the world (tragedy).

Tragedy with a twist!

In tragic theatre, the story typically ends with the hero dying or coming to some horrible end because he has made the wrong choice (because he has learned too late the lessons from his experience). However, the genre does leave open the possibility that the tragic hero can make the right choice and create a different ending. Rebecca Bushnell (2016) explains that central to the genre of tragedy is how we experience choice and consequences in an enacted present that may challenge our understanding of the past. She describes the opportunity for a tragic hero to resist entrapment in his own story by actively writing the future of the story, rather than being trapped in a sense of fate or predetermined destiny.

Bushnell's description of tragic choice challenges the conventional view of tragedy based on the premise that the hero's choice is defined by his character (and a fatal flaw) and instead suggests that the hero's choices can in fact define the character differently. In other words, tragic characters can become what they choose. Bushnell (2016) refers to Macbeth, when Banquo asks the sisters whether they "can look into the seeds of time / And say which grain will grow and which will not". Bushnell (2016) notes that "the image of the 'seeds of time', some of which sprout and some which do not, suggests that the future is not fixed; rather, alternative stories are latent in that soil of existence" (line 574). – "freeing voices and possibilities that were always already there" (line 910), allowing freedom of choice even though still within limits.

Bushnell's interpretation of tragedy as encompassing an opportunity for the hero to make a choice that allows him to avoid his tragic fate is the version of the genre that I believe has the most to offer people in conflict. Though sometimes people in conflict have made a bad and irreversible choice and have to live with the consequences, at least we can support them in learning from that experience and their suffering. However, at other times, when we have the opportunity to support them early enough in their story, they may be able to make more informed choices and avoid a tragic fate – we can help them rewrite their conflict story into a "tragedy with a twist".

What would a tragic conflict story look like?

Compared with a melodramatic conflict story, a tragic conflict story is one that:

- Is more complex (contains more information and more detail; has more nuanced descriptions of characters and events);

- Admits uncertainty (acknowledges that not everything can be known, that there are gaps and inconsistencies that the storyteller may not be able to explain);
- Acknowledges the complexities of what causes conflict (moves away from simplified and individualised attributions of blame, considers all parties' as well as historical and contextual contributions to the conflict);
- Recognises that the storyteller has made choices in the past and has choices in the future;
- Involves the storyteller taking active steps to try to improve their situation themselves and to embrace change and opportunities for learning and growth.

It is important to acknowledge that re-imaging one's conflict story through the genre of tragedy does not necessarily mean that the conflict will be resolved. It will, however, provide the storyteller with a more realistic and nuanced understanding of the various factors that gave rise to the conflict and support the storyteller in identifying, evaluating, and implementing choices for managing their own future. Sometimes, this may result in a significant plot twist in which the conflict is resolved and life improves for everyone. Other times, the best the storyteller can achieve is learning from their mistakes and, it is hoped, being able to avoid making those same mistakes in the future.

Angela's story rewritten

Let's imagine how Angela's story might be told in a tragic genre:

> I recently faced some challenges dealing with my colleague Georgia. She frequently commented about my university degrees and seemed to challenge my capacity to do the job. Georgia doesn't have a university degree, but she has been in her role for more than 25 years, and so she is very experienced. I, on the other hand, have little experience but two degrees. Most of the staff in the organisation are younger and have at least one degree. Georgia is the oldest staff member and the only one who hasn't had a university education. She must feel rather threatened by that, despite the fact that she has more experience than many of us combined!

I realised, after thinking through it, that I may have contributed to Georgia's apparent dislike of me. She was one of the people on my interview panel, and during my interview I sold myself on the basis that I had TWO degrees, so I was kind of doubly valuable to the organisation. I realise now that while that probably did help me get the job, it also probably felt to Georgia like I was twice as much of a threat, or that I had twice the ego, of other employees who only had one degree. I also realise that I probably kind of "rubbed her nose" in that when I arrived on the first day with my two degrees in frames under my arms. I was ready to hang them on my office walls (even though, as it turned out, I only got a workstation in a shared area, not an actual office)! That probably explains her comments during my induction about whether or not I wanted her office!

At first I struggled to manage Georgia's behavior. I took it personally and felt that she really didn't respect what I had to offer to the organisation. However, I came to see that Georgia probably felt the same way about me in a weird kind of way – perhaps I never really made her feel that I valued her years of experience and what I could learn from her.

Once I started to understand how Georgia must be feeling, I started to feel a bit sorry for her. It must be hard being the oldest person in the firm and being surrounded by lots of younger people with degrees and huge egos!

I started to think of how I could approach Georgia differently, to see whether I could get her on-side. I began starting conversations with her by saying, "Georgia, this is one of those situations where my theoretical knowledge isn't enough. Can you help me with some of your practical experience?" Once she started to believe that I really wanted to learn from her and that I did value her experience, boy, did it make a difference to our working relationship! Now, some of my colleagues even refer to me as "Georgia's pet"!

Kevin's story rewritten

Let's reconsider Kevin's story in a tragic genre:

So maybe Bill is a bit of a jerk and his behaviour has been less than perfect. But I wonder, in hindsight, what I could have done differently.

I really did believe that I was certain to get the promotion. Perhaps I wasn't that realistic about it. Maybe I was so confident that I didn't put enough effort into the application as I should have. I probably should ask for some feedback from the selection panel about the areas in which they felt that I needed to improve, so at least next time I apply I'll have a better chance.

I also realise that I probably haven't handled my interactions with Bill very well since he took over as team leader. I was against him from the start, because I felt that he had unfairly taken what was meant to be my role. I was pretty negative about everything he did and no doubt he noticed that. When our communication really started to get hostile, I probably should have tried to talk to him about it and clear the air. But I just tried to avoid him. This helped in the short term but probably made things worse in the long term as not only did our communication not improve, it actually got worse.

I'm not sure whether it's too late now to repair our working relationship. It might be worth a try, but I also need to be realistic that he may not be interested. I am going to have to suck it up, either way, in the short term, because I need to keep my job. I guess I have to come up with some strategies to work with him as best as I can until an opportunity comes up for a transfer, or a new job. I might need to talk to my manager to let her know that I'd be interested in making a move if something comes up. I wonder if I should talk to her about Bill's and my communication problems, without making a formal grievance. She might have some suggestions about how we could manage it a bit better. This yelling and shouting isn't good for either of us, or the team as a whole.

I guess worst-case scenario is that things don't get better and I just need to manage working with someone who now hates my guts. It's not ideal, but I guess there are things I can do to minimise the impact that has on me and try not to take it home with me at the end of the day.

The benefits of a tragic conflict narrative

In contrast to the melodramatic conflict narrative, a tragic conflict narrative broadens our thinking about conflict, it opens up new choices for managing it effectively, and it motivates us to face the reality of our situation (so that we are not stagnating while waiting for an unachievable idealistic outcome). Most important, it helps us to learn and grow from our conflicts, whether or not – and however – they might be resolved.

In the following chapter we will consider what is required to shift a melodramatic conflict story into a tragic genre, in terms of how the content of the story needs to change. We will also examine the process of facilitating that shift and, in particular, the role of the coach in supporting people to make that transition.

Notes

1 There are examples of female heroes, including Antigone, Medea, and Hecuba in *The Trojan Women* and Clytemnestra and Phaedra.
2 Ironic reversals occur in comedy, too, but these are the opposite from tragedy – we expect disaster but instead the character experiences a rise in fortune.

REFERENCES

Aristodemou, M. 2000. *Law and literature: journeys from her to eternity.* Oxford: Oxford University Press.

Booth, S. 1983. *King Lear, Macbeth, indefinition, and tragedy.* New Haven, CT: Yale University Press.

Brereton, G. 1968. *Principles of tragedy: a rational examination of the tragic concept in life and literature.* London: Routledge & Kegan Paul.

Bushnell, R. 2016. *Tragic time in drama, film and videogames: the future in the instant.* London: Palgrave Macmillan.

Cawthorn, S. 2013. *Bounce forwards: how to transform crisis into success.* Milton, QLD, Australia: Wiley.

Frye, P. H. 1922. *Romance and tragedy.* Boston: Forgotten Books.

Heilman, R. B. 1968. *Tragedy and melodrama: versions of experience.* Seattle: University of Washington Press.

Leech, C. 1969. *Tragedy.* London: Methuen & Co.

Mandel, O. 1961. *A definition of tragedy.* New York: New York University Press.

Miller, A. 1978. *The collected essays of Arthur Miller.* London: Bloomsbury.

Williams, R. 1966. *Modern tragedy.* London: Chatto & Windus.

8

THE SHIFT FROM MELODRAMA TO TRAGEDY

In this chapter we will look at how our capacity to manage conflict improves when a melodramatic conflict story is developed into a tragic one. We will review the main shifts that a melodramatic conflict story needs to make to enable the protagonist to develop a tragic sensibility and a more constructive approach to conflict. This will then lead us into Part 2 of the book, in which we explore each of the shifts in more detail, and introduce the REAL Conflict Coaching System as a process to facilitate these shifts.

Though it may be possible for a person in conflict to review their own conflict story by engaging in a process of self-reflection and to develop their version of events into one that is more nuanced and leads to more options for constructive conflict management, people usually need support to be able to shift their thinking about their conflict. Melodramatic conflict stories tend to be self-perpetuating, in that the more people tell them, the more they become caught up in a cycle of reinforcing the coherence and integrity of their own stories rather than working to improve the situation (Cobb, 2000–2001).

DOI: 10.4324/9781003128038-8

Other narrative scholars have suggested methods to support people caught up in dysfunctional conflict narratives in rewriting their conflict story into a more constructive version. Some provide advice for narrative approaches to mediation (Cobb, 2000–2001; Winslade and Monk, 2001) and others for narrative approaches to conflict coaching (Jones and Brinkert, 2008). All approaches are based on the premise that the first step is to destabilise, deconstruct, or open up the parties' conflict narratives, before supporting them to create a more constructive conflict story (or, in the case of mediation, supporting both people to co-create a new story together).

The approach suggested in this book is consistent with these other models, and using the genre of melodrama and tragedy as exemplars of the dysfunctional and more constructive stories provides additional and intuitive guidance as to what areas to focus on in the deconstruction and reconstruction process.

Supporting a client to reframe their melodramatic conflict story into a tragic genre has additional benefits. Firstly, it provides the client with an opportunity to develop a more nuanced understanding of the situation, with all of its complexity and uncertainties. This is generally a more realistic foundation upon which to base future choices than an overly simplified and incomplete version of events. This complexity can be developed in relation to the characters involved in the story, the events giving rise to the conflict, and the context in which those events occur. It also encourages the client to move away from simplified attributions of blame and to consider their own contributions to and responsibility for the situation. It helps clients let go of the desperate hope for dream justice and the associated requirement for dependence on others.

In addition, the tragic genre emphasises a move towards the future (rather than a return to the status quo) and a path built on multiple possibilities and choices, requiring self-determination and independence. Though in some cases those choices may be constrained, recognising that there is even limited choice can be empowering. Depending on the circumstances of the particular client, it may even be possible to rewrite the ending into a story of overcoming, into a comedy or romance; however, the foundations for these genres are not found in melodrama – they require the examination and self-reflection of tragedy to create that opportunity. The tragic genre also, importantly, emphasises learning – even where the outcome of the story is something less than ideal, where it truly is a tragedy; despite the client's suffering all is not necessarily lost – something can be gained from the situation.

Six main shifts

Table 8.1 provides a summary of the six main shifts from melodrama to tragedy.

Outcomes of shifting from melodrama to tragedy

Some of the potential consequences of a person developing their melodramatic conflict story into a tragic one could include the following:

The person realises that there is actually no conflict (i.e., the conflict existed in the melodramatic story, but upon rewriting the conflict actually disappeared)

For example, Ping initially presents a story about a conflict she is having with Mary, her supervisor. She explains how Mary is constantly interfering

Table 8.1 The six main shifts from melodrama to tragedy

Shift	Melodrama	Tragedy with a twist
Simplified–complex	Simplified plot	Complex and nuanced version of events
	One-dimensional, morally polarised characters	Complex, internally divided characters
	Focus on characters' actions	Explore characters' intentions
	Individualised and externalised blame	Acknowledgement of conflicting imperatives, social and contextual factors, mutual contributions
Certainty–uncertainty	Certain, coherent version of events	Recognise, acknowledge, and accept uncertainty; develop curiosity
Passive–active	Passive protagonist, submitting to an outcome	Recognise own past actions and choices, prepare for future action and choices, build capacity for self-determination
Dependence–agency	Reliance on others, helpless and dependent.	Take control of own situation, become empowered and independent
Past–future	Focus on the past and a return to it through dream justice	Plan for a better future, embrace change, paradoxical union of victory and defeat
Suffering–learning	Suffering, conflict is something that upsets the moral order	Experience as the foundation for learning and growth, conflict as an opportunity for improvement

with her work, making unwanted suggestions, providing unsolicited feedback, and even going so far as to reach over her shoulder to correct something she was doing on the computer one day. Ping explains how she feels that Mary is constantly undermining her and that Mary thinks she (Ping) is useless in her role and that she (Mary) has to do everything for her. After we go through a process of unpacking the story, filling in gaps, looking for additional information, identifying potential inconsistencies and assumptions, and reviewing Ping's previous choices, actions, and inactions, Ping comes to a startling realisation. Ping suddenly understands that, actually, Mary's interventions are generally quite helpful. Her suggestions and feedback have assisted Ping to improve her work. Though sometimes her manner in providing this assistance has not been ideal from Ping's perspective, Ping acknowledges that she has never really asked Mary whether she could help her in a slightly different way. Ping also realises that, instead of thinking that Ping is hopeless, it is quite possible that Mary thinks that she has potential and her intention is to help Ping to improve and develop. Upon deconstructing her melodramatic conflict story, Ping's rewritten story is no longer one of conflict in which Mary thinks she is hopeless and is intentionally undermining her. The story is now one of opportunity, in which she plans to approach Mary for some direct feedback on her performance to date and to discuss with her how she would like to receive assistance from Mary in relation to her future work.

The person realises that though there is, or has been, a conflict, the conflict does not affect them as much as they previously thought (i.e., the suffering existed in the melodramatic story, but upon rewriting the suffering actually disappeared)

In Angela's story, for example, Georgia's behaviour in frequently using the word "university" or "degrees" when talking with Angela in order to deliberately make her feel inferior to her was the source of great suffering, making Angela perceive her work as a "constant battle" and a "nightmare". After exploring Angela's story in more detail, she realised that in many ways Georgia was feeling threatened by her and in fact felt the same way about almost every other staff member. She identified that Georgia was now one of the oldest staff members and one of the very few who did not have a university degree (let alone two degrees, like Angela). She acknowledged that with recent talk of redundancies, and with Georgia's age and lack of formal qualifications, she must have been feeling particularly vulnerable, which might explain her behaviour. We also explored why Georgia's use of the words "university" and "degrees" acted as such a trigger for Angela, giving rise to uncomfortable emotions. The more we explored the reasons for Angela's suffering, the more Angela started to realise that she wasn't feeling the same way about those words anymore. In fact, she said that she had actually started to feel sorry for Georgia and that in the future when she said those words, Angela was likely to hear it more as Georgia saying, "I feel vulnerable that I don't have a degree and because I haven't been to university", not as a criticism of Angela for having had that opportunity. Angela realised that those words were no longer the source of suffering for her.

The person realises that there is a conflict but that the conflict is more complex or different than previously thought, and the new story opens up different possibilities for managing the situation than previously acknowledged (i.e., in the melodramatic story the client was stuck, but upon rewriting the story the person realises there are multiple choices for action)

In Claire's story, for example, she could only see two possible outcomes – either Alison is somehow forced to move out or Claire would have to continue to suffer for another three months. However, during our coaching session, Claire began to realise that there were other options. She acknowledged that she could, potentially, have a conversation with Alison about sharing food. She recognised that she could perhaps set some clear rules and expectations about food sharing in the house. Claire identified some possible alternatives: that they not share food at all, that food sharing might be okay if they asked each other first, or that they only share certain kinds of foods (items like salt, pepper, tea, milk) that they jointly purchased. Claire also considered some "left field" choices. She wondered whether they might be able to agree to take turns cooking the evening meal, as she and Emma used to do. Along with considering a range of possible choices in relation to food sharing, Claire thought about other aspects of being flatmates that could be discussed and agreed upon with Alison. She talked about some other concerns about the replacement of items such as toilet paper and cleaning products and recognised that she and Alison had never really had a conversation about how these things should be managed. She realised that there were other aspects of their relationship as flatmates that had not been properly clarified and that could be improved, not just the presenting problem of food sharing.

The person realises that there is a conflict and that they have limited choices; however, they recognise that they need to make choices and take action based on the existing situation instead of waiting for someone to save them (i.e., in the melodramatic story the client was waiting for someone to hand down dream justice, but upon rewriting the story the person realises that dream justice is highly unlikely or impossible and that waiting for this is counterproductive and just prolonging their suffering)

Another client of mine, Hazel, presents her story as one in which she is being bullied by her team leader. As we explore her story in more detail and from different perspectives, it seems that this may well be one of those situations in which the melodramatic genre fits rather well. It does seem that her team leader is deliberately acting in a way designed to control and demoralise Hazel, for no good reason. Hazel has approached her manager for support with this situation but was discouraged from making a formal grievance. She was more or less told to "toughen up" and that if she couldn't get along with people she should consider looking for a new job. Her manager also implied that if she chose to take the matter further, word would get around and that she might find it difficult to get another job in this close-knit and small local industry. Hazel has some difficult choices to make. For various reasons, she does not want to take the matter further by making a formal complaint. She knows that she is legally in the right, but she doesn't feel strong enough emotionally to fight that battle, and she is worried that, unfair though it might be, it really could affect her reputation in the local area and may create challenges for her in the future. We explore each of these in some detail, considering the potential risks and benefits of each. She eventually decides that she will start looking for a new job, without making a complaint against her team leader. She recognises that this is not the ideal outcome and that it is unfair, but on talking it through in detail she is now confident that it is the best choice for her in the circumstances.

The person realises that although dream justice may well be possible, the new story helps them understand that dream justice actually comes at a cost and that the negative consequences of 'winning' may actually outweigh the benefits

George is the deputy manager of a large social services agency, run by a major church. George has been in a long-term same-sex relationship with his partner Nico, and this is known and accepted by George's colleagues. The current CEO recently announced his intention to retire at the end of the year, and the agency advertised for a replacement. The obvious candidate for the job was George, who had acted in that role often over the past few years. However, when George applied for the position, he was called aside for a quiet word with the retiring CEO. The CEO indicated to George that the church board (who would be interviewing and appointing the new CEO) had discussed the fact that George has an "un-Christian" lifestyle and had suggested that he withdraw his application for the CEO position. He explained that this would be the best thing to do in the circumstances, because even if George were interviewed and was found to be the most qualified candidate, the board would never appoint him to the position. George received some legal advice and was informed that if this happened he would almost certainly win if he sued the church under antidiscrimination laws. So it seemed that George's options were to quietly withdraw his application and either have to work under a new CEO (who may not turn out to be as qualified as him for the role), to look for another job at a different agency, or to proceed with his application and if (when) unsuccessful, institute legal proceedings against the church. In the melodramatic conflict story, the latter option was likely to lead to dream justice – the church would be punished for its discriminatory practices and George's virtue would be recognised and his position restored (or at least compensated). However, as we discussed this option, George realised that there were potential downsides to that dream justice that were so significant to him that he could not choose that path. George recognised that in the small town where he lived, such an action would become town gossip in no time at all. This was problematic for George for two reasons: firstly, his parents did not know that he was gay and he would likely be outed to them if he took this action. His father was a very conservative, religious man, who was very ill and George thought that this news could very well kill him. He didn't want to put his relationship with his parents and his father's health at risk. Secondly, George was also religious and had a strong bond with the church (despite the actions of the church board in this situation). George did not want to damage the reputation of the church by publicly embarrassing them in this way. For George, though dream justice was very likely available to him, exploring his story and the complexity and reality of the likely endings made him realise that, for him, dream justice came at an unacceptable cost. He chose to withdraw his application and to start looking for another job at a different agency. Though George was not happy about this, through the process of exploring his story and carefully analysing the implications of different endings he resigned himself to the fact that this choice was the best of some bad options for him in this situation. He also understood that if he wanted to pursue his career further, he would be best looking for roles in secular agencies, not those run by religious institutions.

The person is better prepared to fight for dream justice

It's important to note that, in other circumstances, someone in Hazel's or George's position would decide to proceed with the formal complaint and to fight the battle. In this situation, working with the person to carefully consider their story and to identify challenges and risks can help them better prepare for the forthcoming process. The process of helping a client closely examine their conflict story does not always mean that dream justice is not available, nor that it is not the best option for them. However, it is important to check this out carefully before people put energy and resources into following that course of action. When they decide to pursue the fight for justice, exploring their story in detail can help prepare them for that action and for the challenges and risks that may arise in the process.

Supporting others to make the shift

By now you should be able to see the benefits of people shifting their conflict story from a melodrama to tragedy (with a twist!). However, this is something that is quite difficult for someone in conflict to do on their own. Perhaps if they are experienced at engaging in a process of self-reflection and their emotions are not restricting their capacity to think critically and differently about their experiences, they can make these shifts on their own. However, most people need some support to escape the melodrama of conflict.

In attempting to be the catalyst for someone to rewrite their conflict story we need to be very conscious of the role we are playing. As I mentioned earlier, when someone tells us their conflict story, they have certain expectations about how we should respond to their story. In the following chapter we will explore the different roles we could play once someone shares their conflict story with us.

REFERENCES

Cobb, S. 2000–2001. Creating sacred space: toward a second-generation dispute resolution practice. *Fordham Urban Law Journal* 28: 1017–1033.

Jones, T. and Brinkert, R. 2008. *Conflict coaching: conflict management strategies and skills for the individual.* Los Angeles: Sage.

Winslade, J. and Monk, G. 2001. *Narrative mediation: a new approach to conflict resolution.* San Francisco: Jossey Bass.

Part 2

CONFLICT COACHING TO SUPPORT STORY DEVELOPMENT

9

COACHING TO FACILITATE THE SHIFT

When someone tells us their conflict story, there are a number of ways we might respond. Some of these are more helpful than others. In this chapter we will explore some of the different ways we can respond to a person telling us their conflict story, and I will introduce what I find to be the most helpful support role – that of the coach.

Some people will tell their conflict stories to friends, family, or colleagues with a kind of implied request for help. Others will actively seek that support from managers, coaches, or other professionals. When someone in conflict brings us their conflict story, they are in effect inviting us into their story – in one sense we are the person's audience, but in another sense there is a more explicit invitation to take on a role in the story. When working with people whose conflict story fits the melodramatic conflict narrative, we need to be very careful about the role we adopt in their story and the impact that this may have on that person now and into the future.

Sometimes when people in conflict tell stories about it they are just looking for a sympathetic audience, not someone expected to be able to solve

DOI: 10.4324/9781003128038-9

the problem, just someone who reinforces their virtue and takes their side in the conflict. This is often the stance people would like their friends and family to take in their conflict story. They want them to say, "Yes, of course, you are right, that's so horrible what he has done to you, let me make you a nice cup of tea". Though this response makes them feel less alone and perhaps reduces their suffering somewhat, it usually does little to support them in managing the conflict more effectively.

At other times, when people in conflict come to tell their stories they are looking for more than tea and sympathy. They may be looking for someone to "join their team" against the villain. I see this frequently in workplaces, where an individual with a grievance against another employee begins to talk to their colleagues about the failings of the other employee in an attempt to recruit them onto their side. Again, this may make the person feel more supported in their conflict against the other, but it does little to help them manage their conflict effectively. Instead, it broadens the scope of, and frequently escalates, the conflict.

If the person in conflict sees you as someone who is wiser or more powerful in some way, they are likely to tell you their melodramatic conflict story in a way that invites you to adopt the role of the father figure. This invitation might be explicit – the person may directly ask you to give them advice about what to do, to come up with a solution, or to implement some power you may possess to force the outcome they are looking for. Other times the invitation might be more implicit. If you have the necessary knowledge and power, you may be able to help the person resolve their conflict; however, there are risks of intervening in this way and some downsides in the long term. This father figure role can be quite seductive, and in the first part of this chapter I will explain why we need to avoid it where possible.

It is important, however, to clearly point out that coaching is not always the only or the best intervention to support someone in conflict. There are times when a father figure–type approach is necessary and the right intervention. Where someone is at imminent risk of harm they may need more direct support than a coaching intervention. Where someone is subject to coercive and controlling behaviour by another person, coaching has the potential to make the situation worse and dangerous. Where a person is behaving in a way that is illegal or significantly outside what is expected in a workplace, a direct intervention by a person with authority may be required. Having said this, there are many situations in which a father figure–type approach is not required and there is time and opportunity for a coaching intervention. The benefit of this kind of intervention, when it is possible, is that it provides longer term and broader benefits than a simple conflict resolution process. It creates an opportunity for transformation.

In this chapter I will introduce coaching as a way to support someone in conflict, as an alternative to providing a sympathetic audience, joining the person's side against the villain, or having to solve the problem for them. I will also show that this role is not entirely inconsistent with the melodramatic conflict narrative – its foundations can be found in the bumbling helper character (introduced in Chapter 2).

Virtue's helpers

In melodrama, the heroine has two main helpers: the father figure and the bumbling helper. Both of these characters are virtuous, but they differ greatly in their power and influence over the other characters. The father figure is the most powerful character in melodrama. He holds the power to dispense dream justice – by recognising the heroine's virtue, punishing the villain's evil actions, and restoring moral order. The bumbling helper, on the other hand, holds very little power other than moral power. He fully supports the heroine and never doubts her virtue, but in relation to stopping her suffering he is practically useless.

The father figure

In the melodramatic conflict story, where the protagonist is seeking support from someone identified as a potential "father figure", the protagonist must first gain sympathy from them to demonstrate their right to that support. Protagonists must convince the father figure of their virtue and their undeserved suffering to gain sympathy and motivate the father figure to act on their behalf. This activity is inherently linked with disempowerment. To gain the perceived power of another, the protagonist must overtly and incontrovertibly present themselves as completely disempowered; otherwise, they leave themselves open to the response "Why don't you fix it yourself?" The story must make this an impossibility so that the father figure simply must act to maintain his virtue (or risk being recast as one of the villain's henchmen).

Clients who have cast themselves in the melodramatic protagonist role are likely to present to a conflict support person looking for someone to solve their problem for them. They often feel helpless and are desperate for advice or for someone to intervene on their behalf. However, it is important that the conflict support person does not fall into the trap of taking on the role of father figure, because this comes with significant risks. Firstly, it burdens the support person with the responsibility for solving the client's problem. Secondly, it is highly likely that the client has only presented certain aspects of the conflict situation to the support person, so any advice given or action taken by the support person is likely to be based on incomplete and potentially distorted information. There are risks in intervening (either by providing advice or more active involvement in the conflict) based on a narrow interpretation of events by one of the people involved. The conflict support person will not have access to all of the information that might be available and relevant or may misinterpret what they have been told based on their own biases, knowledge, or experience. The conflict support person inevitably becomes part of the conflict (even if the support person believes they are resolving it) rather than helping the other person manage it themselves. Thirdly, and perhaps most important, by adopting the father figure role, the conflict support person reinforces the client's helplessness and makes it less likely that the client will become empowered to manage the situation on their own. The father figure's role as protector of the protagonist is based on the premise that the protagonist is someone in need of protection. Thus, the father figure's role reinforces the fact that the client is unable to control their own destiny. The melodramatic conflict narrative reinforces the client's relative powerlessness and need for the assistance of the father figure and other authoritative figures.

A father figure approach to supporting a client in conflict often leads to dynamics in which the client feels that they are under investigation. They frequently feel judged, become defensive, and actively work to promote their virtue. This can lead to them further embedding their conflict story into the melodramatic conflict narrative.

Adopting the father figure role can be seductive. It is validating to feel that someone values our advice and it is rewarding to feel that we could help someone. We are also culturally predisposed to value knowledge and to be able to share information. People who are trying to help others solve a conflict may have the best intentions to try to provide support by asking questions rather than telling the other one what to do. However, in many cases, these questions resemble disguised recommendations, rather than curious inquiries (Schein, 2013). For example, when someone asks, "Did you talk to them about it?" this implies that in the questioner's opinion that was an option. However, telling someone what to do, even if well-intentioned and good advice, perpetuates dependency and helplessness. It disempowers the other by implying that they do not know or cannot figure out what they are told.

As Baruch Bush and Folger (1994) point out, we can often do better than simply resolving people's conflict for them – we can build their capacity to manage their own conflict now and into the future; we can empower them. Bush and Folger define empowerment as a person's awareness of their own self-worth and the ability to deal with whatever difficulties they face regardless of external constraints. Though the heroine in melodrama may have an awareness of her own self-worth (or virtue), she has very little ability to deal with her difficulties. When people in conflict feel as though they have no control over the situation, their natural response is to look for someone who they think has this control to help them. They want some-one to make the other person change (or go away), or at the very least they want someone to tell them what they should do. Ironically, the more oth-ers provide them with the solution, the more disempowered they become. Where people are provided with opportunities to develop empowerment during their attempts to manage or resolve a conflict (i.e., to increase their confidence, awareness, skills, and decisiveness), these benefits can extend beyond the immediate conflict to the people's future activities, *even when the immediate conflict is not resolved*.

The bumbling helper

The bumbling helper in melodrama has an important role in making the heroine suffer a little less in the situation she has been placed in by the vil-lain. Her helper is there for her, providing moral support, if not practical assistance. The bumbling helper does not require the heroine to demon-strate her virtue before he supports her. He unquestioningly accepts her and is not swayed by others' comments to the contrary (particularly what the villain says about her). He steadfastly sticks by her, through thick and thin, always believing in her and never judging her. He always treats her with unconditional positive regard (Rogers, 1959).

Though the bumbling helper may not be able to save the heroine, his presence may create an environment in which the heroine may start to develop some strength to help herself. Imagine that the heroine has been imprisoned alone in a dark dungeon. In an isolated environment, with nobody to sympathise with her fate or to talk to about what is happening, she is likely to succumb to a helpless despair. However, if imprisoned with her helper, she may feel a little bit better than if she were there alone. Though her helper may not be able to find a way to help her escape, he can in a sense share her burden by being with her. In addition, he presents someone for the heroine to talk to. As she talks to her helper about what has happened, she may also start thinking and talking about how she might escape the situation. In doing so, and particularly if the helper is rather clueless, she may need to explain things to him in some detail, so that he understands. As she attempts to explain more clearly what has led to this situation and what possibilities there may be to escape it, she may also start to see more clearly herself and to come up with new, or more nuanced, strategies for managing the situation better in the future. Her helper's presence may also motivate her to take more action than she might have had she been alone. She may be motivated to live up to her helper's image of her by not seeming too pathetic or unworthy.

A bumbling helper approach to working with a client in conflict is much more likely to result in the client opening up and being willing to consider different ways of looking at the situation without feeling judged or defensive. Clients are usually more than happy to help someone who seems motivated to really understand their experience. They willingly provide more information to explain things in such a way that their confused helper can understand and, in doing so, they frequently improve their own understanding.

Though it seems counterintuitive for a conflict support professional to be presenting themselves as a bumbling helper, this strategy can be particularly useful in the coaching role and echoes sentiments of unconditional positive regard, a client-centred framework, maximising self-determination and empowerment, and humble inquiry (Schein, 2013). I am not suggesting that it is possible to coach someone in conflict without any particular skills or process. Simply bumbling around with nothing more than good intentions is likely to cause more harm than good. As the saying goes, there's no point jumping into a river to save someone who is drowning if you can't swim. What I am saying, however, is that adopting some of the attributes of the bumbling helper (for example, appearing confused and asking for clarification of what the protagonist is saying and reinforcing that as a coach there is nothing you can do outside the coaching session that will resolve the client's concerns) will enhance your ability to support the client within a strong framework of conflict coaching skills and process.

Though the coach may begin their role in the client's conflict story as the bumbling helper, the coach effectively works towards removing themselves from the story altogether. As the client begins to make the shift from melodramatic victim to tragic hero, the client develops the awareness and independence to effectively "go it alone". The coach effectively facilitates the client's process of self-reflection. The coach shifts from being a character in the client's story (the bumbling helper) to the audience of the client's tragic soliloquy.

Comparing roles

Let's consider a simple example to compare the father figure and the bumbling helper roles. In high school, I struggled in my mathematics class. I was an impatient student and tended to rush through the sequence of steps required to work out complicated equations. Doing my homework one evening at the kitchen table, I had attempted one of the set mathematical problems but my answer was incorrect. In frustration, I said to my mother, "I'm so hopeless at maths, I can't do it!"

My mother had two options about how to respond. She could have looked at my work and pointed out where in the steps I had made an error, allowing me to fix it, thus rescuing me from my immediate dilemma and frustration. However, had she done this, what do you think I would have done next time my answer was incorrect? I would likely have immediately called out for my mother to help me again, because she had already demonstrated to me clearly that she could help me solve my problems when I could not.

Alternatively, my mother could have looked at my work and expressed curiosity about it. She could have asked, "Okay, so what are you trying to do here?" and "What steps did you take to do that?" and "What steps did your teacher tell you to take?" These kinds of questions were likely to make me look more closely at what I had attempted to do and probably identify where I had gone wrong in the process. Though my mother had facilitated this looking, she had not directly pointed out where I went wrong or what I could do to fix it. I had done this by myself, with my mother's support. This process was likely to lead to quite a different response next time I was stuck. I would probably ask myself the same kinds of questions that my mother had asked me the previous time, and chances are I would identify for myself my error and the solution without having to call my mother to help me. I would probably also feel rather self-satisfied at having resolved the problem myself this time – I would feel empowered.

Here's another example of how taking the bumbling helper role can have significant long-term positive consequences on people in conflict. A few years ago I worked with a group of team leaders of a large federal government agency. They were complaining that they spent a large proportion of their time trying to sort out conflict between members of their teams. Team members would frequently come into their offices to complain to them about another team member's behaviour, and they would have to go and intervene. Their normal approach was that of the "father figure" – they would either tell the staff member what they should do to solve their conflict or they would actively intervene by talking with the other person on the staff member's behalf.

I trained the team leaders in a simplified form of conflict coaching. They implemented the process as the first step to managing conflict when a team member came to them with a conflict problem they wanted resolved. At first there was some resistance to the coaching process, particularly that team leaders felt that it was more time-consuming to spend 30–40 minutes taking their team member through the process than simply telling the team members what they should do. In the early stages of implementation, team members also resisted the process, some suggesting that team leaders were absolving themselves from their management responsibilities by not managing team conflict. However, after a couple of months, the team leaders started to observe a shift in their team members' behaviour. As the team members became familiar with the coaching process and the kinds of questions that their team leaders were likely to ask them when they brought a conflict problem to them, team members started to present to their team leaders with pre-prepared answers to these typical questions. This already seemed like a step in the right direction – team members were thinking about things in more detail prior to going to the team leader for help.

After another few months, the team leaders became worried because fewer and fewer staff were coming to them with conflicts. The team leaders suspected that conflicts were going "underground" because staff did not want to have to go through the coaching process. However, after some further investigation, quite a different story emerged. What had actually started happening was that team members, in preparing for the coaching process, realised that they did not need the team leader to take them through it. They could identify the relevant information, evaluate different choices about how to manage it, and implement their decision themselves. Not only had staff learned how to self-manage conflict but they had also started to implement some of the strategies at an earlier stage in the conflicts, so that many conflicts were now being dealt with early and in a constructive manner. Staff morale began to increase and teams worked more effectively together.

Team leaders, by refusing to take on the father figure role, and yet not abandoning their staff to their own means altogether, effectively took on a kind of melodramatic bumbling helper role. They sat alongside their staff and supported them in exploring different possible ways to manage the conflict themselves, in a safe and supportive environment. This is not to say that sometimes the team leaders did need to step in and take a more authoritative and directive role – this was sometimes necessary in the circumstances. However, the important shift was that this was no longer the default response.

Who makes a good coach?

Somewhat counterintuitively, it is harder to coach someone you know well than someone who is a complete stranger. This is because when you know someone well you have already established your own ideas about what kind of person they are, how they typically behave in certain situations, and what is important to them. When we think we know these things, we are less likely to ask questions about them, which means that the client has fewer opportunities to reflect on those things themselves.

A good coach needs to have a growth mindset when it comes to people in conflict, truly believing that everyone can learn and improve their conflict management skills with the right support. A good coach also needs to be able to interact with their clients in a nonjudgemental way, showing them unconditional positive regard.

A good coach needs to understand that the stories clients tell them about their conflicts are never entirely true or complete. They need to be able to support the client to explore the client's story without getting caught up in it themselves. They need to understand that there will always be things that they do not know about the client's conflict situation, either because the client does not disclose them or because the client does not themselves know about or acknowledge them.

A good coach is genuinely curious and interested in understanding clients' experiences. However, they recognise that the purpose of coaching is not for the coach to understand. Rather, the coach is simply there to facilitate the client's better understanding of their own experiences. This can happen even when the coach does not fully understand the client's situation. The coach's role is to prompt the client to think differently from the way they would if they were simply reflecting alone.

A good coach wants to help others to help themselves. They need to be able to let go of their own ideas of what is right or best for their clients and support their clients to make their own choices. The coach fosters the client's empowerment and self-determination. In one sense, the coach aims to make themselves redundant – providing just enough support so that the client can continue on their own.

The primary role of the coach is to provide the opportunity for clients to learn from their own experience. The coach is not teaching the client (as a trainer may do), nor are they providing advice (as a lawyer may do), nor are they trying to find out what really happened (as an investigator may do), nor are they trying to find out who is right or wrong (as a judge may do). They are listening and asking questions so that the client can learn from talking through their situation and thinking about it more deeply in a supportive setting.

Coaching skills

To effectively support a client in shifting their conflict story from melodrama to tragedy, there are some fundamental skills a coach requires.

Firstly, the coach needs to be able to create a safe space for the client to engage in self-reflection. Secondly, the coach needs to have excellent listening skills. Thirdly, the coach needs to be able to ask appropriate questions at the right time. Fourthly, the coach should use the client's language where possible and nondirective language at all times.

Creating a safe space for self-reflection

The coach must be able to create a safe space for the client to engage in self-reflection. At times coaching can be uncomfortable for the client. Clients typically experience moments that are important for shifting the story but are not easy. Clients may feel overwhelmed, as what they had thought of as a simple (if frustrating) situation becomes more complex; they may become emotional as they process different aspects of their experiences and choices; they may be embarrassed or ashamed when they consider more carefully their role in the conflict. The coach needs to be able to support the client through these challenging moments so that they stay engaged in the process.

The coach must ensure that the coaching process is as confidential as possible, so that the client feels safe sharing information that may be very personal or make them appear less virtuous. Though complete confidentiality may not be guaranteed (for example, if the client discloses information that leads the coach to think someone's life may be in danger, the coach may have a legal obligation to share that information with someone else), the client should feel comfortable being open and honest. In situations in which the coach is not entirely independent (e.g., where the person coaching is the "client's" line manager), any limitations on confidentiality should be made clear and agreed upon by all involved before any coaching starts.

The coach should consistently maintain unconditional positive regard towards the client. If the coach finds this difficult for some reason (e.g., the client is discussing something that is strongly against the coach's values), the coach should withdraw from the coaching relationship and, if possible, refer the client to another coach.

Listening

Though most people believe that they are good listeners, the way that we listen in a coaching context is very different from how we listen in other situations. In coaching, we are listening to understand the client's experience, not to have a conversation, problem-solve, or argue. We are listening to *what* is being said and *how* it is being said (for example, the language being used and the structure of the client's conflict story). We are also listening for what is unsaid (for example, where the client avoids talking about their own actions or does not discuss what happens in between recounted events).

We are listening with empathy, not judgement. We are listening with curiosity. We are listening for opportunities for the client to think differently and more deeply about their experiences. We are listening for what the client knows, what they are assuming, and what they do not know. We are listening for missing information, gaps in the story, inconsistencies, uncertainties, choices (taken or unnoticed), and possibilities.

Questioning

Much of what the coach does in a coaching session is ask questions. However, we are not asking questions to gather facts; we are not investigating "what really happened" or "who is right or wrong". We are asking questions for a particular purpose: to encourage the client to think differently and deeply about their experience.

We ask almost entirely open-ended questions; that is, questions that invite more than a yes/no answer, questions that invite the client to provide more information, to elaborate. We are also careful not to include assumptions in our questioning. For example, when a client complains about something that someone has done to them, instead of asking, "Did you speak to them about it?" we ask, "What did you do after that?" We ask questions that are directly related to what the client is talking about, not questions that we find interesting but that are based on our own train of thought and not the client's.

The coach uses mostly open-ended questions or brief statements that invite the client to provide more information and to keep talking. It's important that in doing so we are *not investigating* or *interrogating* the client's version of events. Rather, we are asking from a place of trying to support the client to better understand, as best we can, the client's experiences leading up to this coaching session.

Language

We use the client's own language as much as possible, rather than paraphrasing or summarising. This builds rapport but also keeps the focus on the client's experience of the conflict using the client's own language, which promotes more authentic self-reflection. For example, our client says, "When he said that he really pissed me off!" instead of saying, "Why did that really annoy you?" we follow up with "Tell me what, exactly, pissed you off about what he said?"

As a coach, we do very little paraphrasing or summarising. Questions and attentive listening are usually sufficient to support the client to reflect on their own experiences. When we paraphrase or summarise, we risk focusing on what we, the listener, think is most important or relevant, and we can divert the client's train of thought towards following our own. If, as a coach, we feel that a short summary might be helpful, we ask the client to provide it. For example, "Could you summarise for me what you just said about the consequences of that conversation?"

Our language is also consistently nondirective. We are careful not to suggest solutions or actions to the client. We always give the client a choice about what they want to talk about and whether they want to answer a question. We promote self-determination and empowerment in the language that we use.

Conclusion

If we are going to effectively help others to become the hero of their own future, we need to let go of our desire to be their hero. Though in some circumstances a client may truly need a father figure to rescue them from a conflict situation, there are also many situations in which people in conflict have the capacity and opportunity to help themselves with a little support from a coach. Effective coaches can distinguish between those two circumstances and, in the former situation, refer their client to another support person who has the power to intervene in a more direct way.

Though a bumbling helper mindset can help a coach stay curious and promote the client's own self-determination, this does not mean that anyone can coach without learning the skills and a coaching process to provide the support that a client in conflict needs. Particularly when a client is in conflict, there are many risks involved if the coach gets it wrong. Coaches need to have a strong understanding of conflict dynamics, a good grounding in a recognised coaching process, and the skills to know when and how to intervene.

REFERENCES

Baruch Bush, R. A. and Folger, J. P. 1994. *The promise of mediation: responding to conflict through empowerment and recognition*. San Francisco: Jossey-Bass.

Rogers, C. 1959. A theory of therapy, personality and interpersonal relationships as developed in the client-centered framework. In Koch, S. (Ed.) *Psychology: a study of a science: Vol. 3. Formulations of the person and the social context*, pp. 184–256. New York: McGraw Hill.

Schein, E. H. 2013. *Humble inquiry: the gentle art of asking instead of telling*. San Francisco: Berrett-Koehler.

10

SIMPLE TO COMPLEX

One of the most important shifts required for a client to move away from a melodramatic conflict story towards the tragic genre is the shift from a simplified presentation of the story to a more nuanced and complex version of events. Simple is easy and comforting, but it is not realistic or helpful when it comes to understanding and managing conflicts. As the client unpacks and expands on their original conflict story, the client's clarity and comprehension are likely to improve, and at the same time the story will likely shift away from melodramatic coherence. This can be an unsettling experience for a client, because incorporating this additional information tends to force them to re-examine things they had thought of as right and certain. It is important that the coach provides a safe and supportive environment for this work.

This shift from simple to complex is the most important one to lay the foundation for better conflict management. The more time we spend with a client in conflict exploring the details of their situation, the better their future choices are like to be and the more they will learn. If we do not

DOI: 10.4324/9781003128038-10

spend enough time exploring and expanding the client's conflict story, the later shifts (discussed in Chapter 8) will either not happen or they will happen in a superficial way. I can't emphasise enough the value of simply getting the client to talk in more detail about what has happened.

The coach can achieve this by maintaining a curious stance and presenting as trying to fully understand the situation from the client's perspective. It's important to start only by supporting the client to fill in gaps (rather than try to correct any inconsistencies or incorporate other perspectives) because any suggestion that you might be challenging the client's story at this point is likely to lead them to become defensive and more likely to revert back to the security of their melodramatic story. The coach should take care to ask questions to develop complexity in the story without judging or questioning the client's perspective. If the coach simply asks for more details about what the client has already told them, from a position of curiosity and wanting to understand better the client's experience, the client is likely to be very willing to elaborate.

Clients almost always know much more about the situation than they share in their initial story. They are often not even aware that they have a lot more information available to them that would assist them to better understand the situation and their choices. The metaphor I like to use for this process is based on the melodramatic conflict story plot as a kind of path of stepping stones. The story starts at a location of idealised past and then the client tends to take me to the present by jumping from stepping stone to stepping stone along the way. The stepping stones often each represent an instance in which the villain does something that causes the client to suffer. In between each of those stepping stones, and around each of those stepping stones, is more landscape that is not included in the original story.

I want to take my client right back to the first stepping stone in the story (the first event). At that point, I want to ask my client to look backwards and tell me a bit more detail about what came before that stepping stone. As we then move slowly forward, through the sequence of stepping stones along the path (heading towards dream justice but with a large obstacle in the way at some point, put there by the villain), I walk alongside my client and slow them down. I ask them to describe to me everything we see along the way. I ask what is going on around each stepping stone; I ask what is going on in between each stepping stone. I ask my client, instead of jumping from stone to stone, to walk very slowly along the path in between them and to have a good look around at all points along the way. We also look for different paths that might exist along the way that the client perhaps didn't notice in her original travels or that she chose not to take. We explore where some of those paths might lead. Some of the paths, in hindsight, may be obvious, but some might be quite overgrown and require quite a lot of exploration to identify.

Figure 10.1 represents the plot of a melodramatic conflict narrative. Each event (shown as circles or stepping stones) is usually an incident in which the villain did something to make the storyteller suffer. The image also shows that the idealised past and the future (dream justice) look the same. Dream justice is a return to the idealised past.

Figure 10.2 represents a more realistic version of events, incorporating more events, people, and choices than were included in the melodramatic story. It also demonstrates the flaws in the imperfect past and the fantasy of dream justice. The image also shows that outside the path of originally described events, there is additional information that may be relevant. There are also many new opportunities for choice, learning, and growth.

When facilitating the shift from simple to complex, there are a number of areas in the client's story that are helpful to explore: adding history and context, identifying specific examples and discussing them in detail, filling in the gaps, clarifying the order of events, developing a nuanced understanding of factors contributing to the conflict, increasing the cast

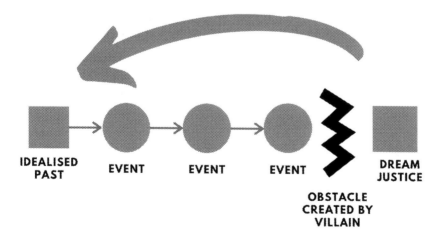

Figure 10.1 The melodramatic conflict narrative plot

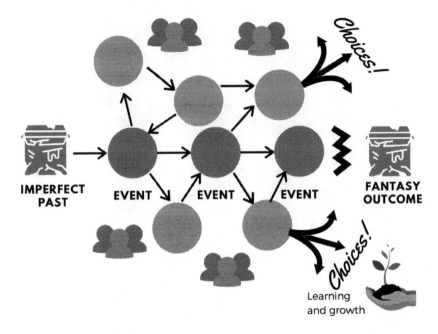

Figure 10.2 Tragic reality

of characters, and developing more complex character portrayals. Each of these are discussed in more detail in this chapter.

Add history and context

Melodramatic conflict stories tend to start with an action by the villain that sets the conflict in motion, upsetting the idealised past. The villain's actions create the main events in the story, and the client's suffering is portrayed as the impact of those actions. However, there is usually more history and context to the conflict that the client does not pay attention to when caught up in the melodrama of conflict. In melodrama, the conflict is all about the client and the villain, and all of the client's suffering is caused by the villain's actions. This narrowing of focus diverts the client's attention from historical and contextual factors that may increase the client's understanding of what led to the conflict arising and/or escalating and that also may provide opportunities for the client to have influence over their own future.

Let's consider now how a coach could add history and content and what impact this might have, by using Angela's conflict story as an example. In

Angela's story, the coach could add some history and context by asking Angela questions about how she came to work in the organisation. Simply asking Angela to talk more about the organisation and what her position entails can sometimes lead the client to pay more attention to information that might turn out to have a bearing on the conflict situation. The coach could also ask for specific details about her first meeting with Georgia (what exactly was said by each of them, what happened next, etc.).

Useful questions in Angela's conflict:

- How did you come to be working in this organisation?
- Tell me about the first time you met Georgia …
- Tell me about that first day when the induction happened …

Let's look at how this line of questioning played out in Angela's coaching session. As I explored the history and context of Angela's conflict story with her, some new information emerged, which lay the foundations for further insights later in the coaching session. For example, Angela explained that she applied for the job in this organisation because it had a reputation for supporting young innovators, and she wanted to work for a company that was full of young people and that supported innovation. She explained that she was short-listed and then interviewed and that she felt that she performed well at the interview and this was confirmed when she was offered the role she had applied for.

I asked her to tell me about the interview. Angela explained that she was interviewed by a panel of four people, the CEO, the human resources manager, one of the young team members, and Georgia. The fact that Georgia was on her interview panel was new information, which may or may not be relevant to Angela better understanding the conflict between them. I asked Angela to describe her experience in the interview (note that I asked this is general terms, rather than going straight to focus on her interactions with Georgia during the interview). Angela explained that each member of the panel seemed to have specific questions allocated to them. She discussed some of the questions that she found easy to answer and some of the more challenging ones. She said that one of the questions Georgia asked her was what she could bring to the role. Angela described her answer as focusing on the fact that she had two degrees, not just one, and so she was kind of doubly qualified for the role. She said that she told Georgia and the panel that her IT qualifications and her MBA together gave her an advantage in fulfilling the role that many others would not have. I asked Angela how she felt the panel responded to her answers. She answered that she felt they were all quite impressed, although she had noticed at the time that Georgia seemed less interested in her degrees – she had asked a follow-up question about Angela's "actual experience", which Angela felt put her on the spot, because she hadn't had that much practical experience at the time.

Already this discussion of Angela's experience during her interview provides us with new information that sets the scene for the later conflict with Georgia. The unpleasant interaction between the two of them during Angela's induction makes a little bit more sense given what happened at the interview.

I asked Angela to tell me about her first day at work, when the induction conversation happened. I took her back to the moment when she first walked in the door and asked her to describe in detail what happened that morning. Angela described greeting the receptionist and someone calling Georgia to come and show her around and to carry out her induction. She discussed meeting some of the other staff and chatting with them (in Georgia's presence) about what degrees they had and what university they went to. She also mentioned in passing that a couple of people noticed that she was carrying two framed certificates. Apparently, she had brought them in to work with her to hang up in her office (although as it turned out she was only given a workstation, so there was no wall to hang them on).

Angela's story started to gather some complexity, and the new information began to set the scene for the future conflict with Georgia. Angela had already recognised that Georgia did not have a university degree and that she was much older than almost all of the other employees. Now we started to see that Georgia's comments during Angela's induction were not quite so "out of the blue" and that some of the things that had happened during Angela's interview and as Georgia took Angela around to meet other employees may have contributed to Georgia reacting in the way she did.

Claire's story about her conflict with Alison provides another useful illustration of this point. Claire's original story did not provide any information about the discussions that she and Alison had prior to Alison moving into her apartment, although it seems highly unlikely that Alison moved in without any further conversations with Claire. Claire's story also did not have any information about whether the conversations she had with Emma (her former "ideal" housemate) when Emma first moved in were different from the conversations she later had with Alison. This could shed some light on Claire's different experiences living with both of them.

Knowing what was said (or left unsaid) between them about sharing food would be very useful in understanding the situation better and perhaps identifying the best course of action to take. For example, if Claire and Alison never had a conversation about sharing food, then this may help explain why Alison does not seem to understand Claire's expectations about that. Also, if Claire has never clearly explained her expectations to Alison, this would help explain why Alison is continuing to use her food. It may open up the possibility that Alison's behaviour could change if she was clearly made aware of Claire's expectations about sharing food. Alison may be able to become a better flatmate in Claire's eyes if she changed her behaviour in this respect, and they may be able to develop a better relationship as flatmates without Alison having to move out.

Discuss specific examples in detail

When telling a melodramatic conflict story, clients usually present interactions in generalisations. For example, they say things like "she always embarrasses me" or "every time she speaks to me she makes smart comments about my degrees". An important part of working with a client's conflict story is to get into the specific details about incidents in their conflict story. In an initial coaching session, I usually ask about three specific examples: the first time something happened, another time something happened, and the last time something happened.

For example, when coaching Angela, I might invite her to "tell me about the first time Georgia said something to you about your degrees or your university education," and then I would ask Angela to provide me with very specific details about that interaction. Exactly when did it take place? Where were you when that interaction happened? Who was around you at the time? What led up to that comment? What exactly did Georgia say? What exactly did you say in response? What happened next?

I would keep in mind that in Angela's melodramatic story, she is likely to describe the situation by telling me what Georgia said and how that made Angela feel (rather than what Angela did or said in response), so I would ask specific questions about Angela's actions. Once she had unpacked the first example in detail (I know if there is sufficient detail if I feel like I just watched a live replay of the conversation on video – I have that level of information about the interaction), I would ask her to describe another time that happened (again, asking questions to get detail). Finally, I would ask about the last time that happened (again, asking lots of questions to unpack the detail).

If I felt comfortable challenging Angela a little at this point, I would also ask for an example of when that didn't happen; for example, "Angela, tell me about a time when you had a conversation with Georgia and she didn't mention your degrees or your university education". In other words, I would assume that there was an exception to what Angela described as happening "every time Georgia talked to her" and ask her to describe it.

Note that the language is important – I did NOT ask whether there was an exception; rather, I assumed that there was and asked the client to describe it. If you ask whether there is an exception, as a yes/no question, the client is likely to automatically say "no" to maintain the internal coherency of their story. However, if you simply ask them to describe an exception, more than likely they will be able to do so.

Fill in the gaps

As depicted in Figure 10.1, a client's melodramatic conflict story will incorporate a few major events, likely to be incidents when the villain did something that made them suffer. The story is likely to omit information about things that happened in between those major dramatic events, even though those less dramatic events may be useful to consider in developing the client's understanding of their current situation. For this reason, it is also helpful to ask the client about things that happened in between the events they have already reported. For example, in Angela's case, a simple question like "What happened between you and Georgia after the induction conversation but before she next mentioned your degrees?" can be useful to identify other relevant events, some context for later events, or, at the very least, a time in which nothing particularly negative happens (which can provide some balance to the overall plot).

Clarify the order of events

As the client's story begins to expand, adding more events and detail, clients can become confused about the order of events. They also often present an initial story in which the events are disorganised (for example, in Angela's story she refers to Georgia constantly making comments about her university degrees prior to describing the induction incident, whereas in fact the induction incident occurred before the university comments started). It can be helpful for clients to clarify the order of events and develop a more accurate chronology, and this also supports the client in identifying and exploring causal links between the events in their story.

Develop a nuanced understanding of factors contributing to the conflict

Angela originally presented the problem in her story as completely caused by Georgia. She did not explicitly or implicitly recognise that she herself, perhaps in addition to some social or contextual factors, may have contributed to the situation. However, exploring the story, Angela recognised a number of factors that may have set the scene for her conflict with Georgia. First, she identified that most other employees in the organisation were considerably younger than Georgia and that Georgia was the only employee without a university degree. She also described how she emphasised the fact that she had two degrees in response to Georgia's question during her interview and that she carried her two degrees in frames into the office on her first day at work (leading up to the induction conversation). She also talked about conversations she had that morning with other employees (in front of Georgia) about their degrees and which universities they attended. Though none of these actions by Angela are blameworthy in any way, they do provide some context for Georgia's behaviour. It does seem possible that Angela unintentionally highlighted to Georgia something that Georgia may be sensitive about (not having a degree) and perhaps added to Georgia's growing sense of unease about her standing in the organisation. It also potentially explains why Georgia seemed to be reacting so badly to Angela (rather than other employees) – because Angela had TWO degrees!

Increase the cast of characters

As I described in Chapter 3, melodramatic conflict stories tend to revolve around two main characters: the protagonist and the villain. However, conflicts usually occur in the presence of other people, who are either observing or involved or impacted in some way by the actions of these two main characters. Focusing the client's attention on people other than the villain can be useful, because considering these characters can often provide different information and perspectives on the conflict.

For example, asking Angela about the other people who work with her and Georgia provided new insight into the situation. While discussing the other staff members and what Angela knew of their backgrounds, it became clear that Georgia was the only employee without a university degree. This discussion also revealed that most of the other staff were much younger and engaged in the workplace in a different way than Georgia (e.g., sending instant messages over Slack instead of having face-to-face conversations). This knowledge provided Angela with new insights into what had been happening and a more nuanced understanding of factors affecting Georgia and Angela in this situation.

Here are some examples of questions to increase the cast of characters in Angela's conflict story:

- Who else do you work with in addition to Georgia?
- Tell me about your other colleagues …
- How do you get along with them?
- How do they seem to get along with Georgia?
- When you and Georgia have those kinds of interactions, who else is usually around to observe them?
- What do other people do when they observe you and Georgia interacting like this?

Develop more complex character portrayals

The coach should support the client to explore simplistic character descriptions, particularly the client's portrayal of themselves as completely virtuous and the villain as entirely evil. The coach should encourage balance in the client's perception of both themselves and others, reinforcing the imperfection of the human condition.

For example, the coach can ask questions that explore what Cobb (2013) calls the "underbelly" (283) of the character traits (in the melodramatic narrative what we would refer to as "virtues") that a client views positively. For example, clients may portray themselves as "organised" without acknowledging the possibility that others may view their behaviour as cold. A discussion about how what one person sees as a virtue (e.g., organisational skills) can be perceived by others quite differently (e.g., as micromanagement or a lack of attention to building relationships with co-workers). Let us say, for another example, that a client described their efficiency as a response to a heavy workload, which left them little time for relationship building. The coach could then draw attention to the client's efforts to balance these two competing priorities and ask questions about what this was like for the client and those impacted by this struggle, which could lead to an opportunity for the client to recognise the complexity and conflict inherent in the situation. Such a line of questioning could provide the impetus for the client to acknowledge their conflicting imperatives, as well as the social and contextual circumstances that drive them, rather than making judgements based on individualised and externalised blame. Questions such as "What are some of the things that affect your ability to be both efficient and caring?" could help "unpack" this feature of the client's narrative (Hardy, 2008, 265–266).

The coach could also ask for examples of times when the "villain" of the client's story did something positive. For example, I might ask Angela to "tell me about a time when Georgia did value your work." Note that I didn't ask whether or not Georgia had ever valued her work — Angela is likely to answer with an automatic "no" to maintain the coherency of her melodramatic conflict story. However, by asking with the assumption that there is such an example, the client will very often provide one!

Much of the work a coach can do to support the client to develop a more complex characterisation of the villain happens in the second shift (from certainty to uncertainty). This is because much of the client's characterisation of the villain is based on uncertain assumptions about the villain's intentions. We will consider this shift in more detail in the next chapter.

Conclusion

The foundations of supporting a client in shifting from a melodramatic conflict story to a more realistic version of events lies in the detail. As a client's story becomes more complex, the story no longer remains coherent, and opportunities open up for different ways of thinking about and responding to the situation. It is surprising, however, how difficult it can be to support people to make this shift. When listening to a person telling their conflict story, it is easy to get caught up in the coherent and morally satisfying version of events without questioning it. As I explained in Chapter 1, human beings are inherently likely to join the dots and fill in the gaps without even noticing what is missing. As a coach supporting someone in conflict, we have to consciously make an effort to remind ourselves of what we don't know (and what the client is therefore not paying attention to and telling us). The more time we spend with a client, nonjudgementally supporting them to add detail and complexity to their version of events, the more likely it is that the client will increase their understanding of the situation and their choices for moving forwards. I cannot emphasise enough how important this shift is. It takes time and effort and often leads to the client feeling rather overwhelmed by all of this new detail, but it is well worth it if you can support the client through this first shift.

REFERENCES

Cobb, S. 2013. *Speaking of violence: the politics and poetics of narrative dynamics in conflict resolution.* New York: Oxford University Press.

Hardy, S. 2008. Mediation and genre. *Negotiation Journal* 24(3): 247–268.

11

CERTAIN TO UNCERTAIN

In conflict situations, feeling certain is almost always going to lead to problems. When we think about our conflict through a melodramatic narrative, we frequently make assumptions and jump to conclusions about things that we do not actually have evidence to support. Shifting from feeling certain about our conflict to recognising and accepting some uncertainty is important for a few reasons: it helps us identify what it is that we actually know, compared with what we are assuming. We can then consider whether and how we might find information to confirm or disconfirm our assumptions. Recognising that there are things that we do not know also opens up new possibilities for understanding and managing our conflict and the other people involved.

Some of the typical things that the protagonist in the melodramatic conflict narrative feels certain about include:

* Their own virtue and lack of contribution to the conflict;
* The villain's evil intentions and blameworthiness;
* That dream justice will give them what they need.

DOI: 10.4324/9781003128038-11

Angela, for example, is convinced that she is a good worker who is well-qualified and able to get along with her colleagues (unless, of course, they are evil villains like Georgia). In her initial presentation of her conflict story, she has no awareness that anything she has done might have contributed to the conflict arising or that there may be more going on here than simply Georgia acting out her dislike of Angela in an unfair way. She is certain that Georgia sees her as a threat and is enjoying making Angela suffer. She uses language like "it clearly shows" to demonstrate this point. She is also certain about what might happen should she try to speak with Georgia about her concerns (Georgia will give some smart answer about how Angela should have learnt how to manage this kind of situation at university) and uses this belief to justify her inability to talk to Georgia about it. Angela is also certain that there are only two solutions to her conflict – either Georgia goes or Angela quits (which she is certain is the unfair outcome).

The illusionary coherency of melodramatic conflict stories supports this artificial certainty. When the recounted events are all examples of the villain acting in a way that makes the protagonist suffer and there are no examples of the protagonist doing anything active to contribute to the conflict or its resolution, the story promotes this sense of certainty. The work of the first shift (from simplicity to complexity) is already opening up some areas of uncertainty or inconsistency in the conflict story and so preparing for this second shift.

Developing uncertainty about the client's virtue and contributions

In the melodramatic conflict narrative, one of the easiest ways for the protagonist to maintain their virtuous character is to set the scene by presenting some of their virtuous qualities and then appear to do (and to have done) nothing active in relation to the conflict. One step towards shifting a client's certainty about their own virtue is simply to *ask about the client's actions*. The example I gave about Bridget (Chapter 4) and her complaints about the emails and text messages that her former boyfriend was sending to her demonstrates this point nicely. Once I asked Bridget to tell me not just how she felt but *what she had done* when receiving those messages it became clear that she had been actively responding. The content of the replies that

Bridget had been sending may have contributed to perpetuating the conflict and at the very least were not helpful in resolving it. Exploring these
in detail allowed Bridget to step away from her role of innocent, passive
victim and realise that she had also acted in a way that, in hindsight, was
not entirely virtuous. This realisation also allowed her to be slightly more
forgiving of her ex-boyfriend's behaviour, because she realised that neither
of them had been acting as their best selves in their interactions.

When coaching a client with a strong sense of righteousness, it can be
helpful to support them to consider *alternative possibilities to their past choices*.
For example, when the client describes an action that they have taken,
the coach can ask them to talk about what their intention was when they
decided to act in that way. The coach can then follow up by asking about
what unintended consequences their action may have had. Highlighting
unintended consequences helps the client realise that they can never be 100
percent certain of the consequences of their actions (past or future). There
are almost always unintended consequences (good or bad) of anything a
client chooses to do. Even if the client cannot think of anything in particular, they may acknowledge the possibility that there were unintended
consequences that they do not know about, again increasing their level of
uncertainty and, hopefully, also their curiosity.

For example, remember when Angela talked about her job interview in
which she made a point about having two degrees? I asked Angela what her
intention was when she made that point. She explained that she wanted
to encourage the panel to give her the job over other applicants with only
one degree. When I asked Angela what might have been some unintended
consequences of her making that point, she thought for a moment and
then conceded that she possibly made Georgia feel even worse than normal
about not having any degree and that this may have set their working relationship off on the wrong foot.

The coach can also ask about *what alternative actions the client could have taken* in
that moment and what the consequences of those different choices might
have been. This line of questioning shifts the client from being certain
about their action as the only thing that they could have done at the time
to a state of uncertainty (by highlighting unintended consequences and
alternatives that the client may not have considered at the time).

For example, when Angela described the conversation she had with
Georgia during her induction when Angela says she was "tongue-tied",

I asked her what it was that made her choose not to say to Georgia what she was thinking in that moment. I then asked her what the consequences of that choice were for her and then what the unintended consequences of that choice were for her. Angela described the intended and positive consequences of her choice as that she was polite and professional in her interaction with Georgia and she didn't escalate the tension between them by reacting strongly to what Georgia said. Angela also acknowledged that some unintended consequences were that she had missed an opportunity to build more of a connection with Georgia by not saying more. As we then talked about what other things Angela could have said instead she recognised that it was hard to know which choice would have led to the best outcome but that there were definitely other choices available to her at the time.

Though Angela cannot go back in time and have that induction conversation over again, what this line of questioning and conversation achieved was that Angela recognised that in any given situation there were multiple choices for what to say and how to say it. This recognition was important later in the coaching session when Angela came to make plans for what actions she might take to improve the situation in the future. Angela was prepared to come up with multiple options for how she might manage her conflict with Georgia and willing to accept that any choice she might make could have unexpected consequences. This made her more likely to critically review her potential future choices and thus feel more confident that the choice she did make was the most likely to achieve her goals. It also meant that she was cautious about "putting all her eggs in the one basket" because she allowed for the possibility that her choice might not go exactly to plan. She recognised that there were always going to be contingencies and factors that she could not know about that might affect the results. This motivated her to consider alternatives and to develop backup plans if her first choice didn't work out as expected.

Support clients to identify assumptions about others' blameworthiness

When clients are stuck in the melodramatic victim role, they are quick to judge others' behaviour and to assume that the reasons behind their actions are deliberate evil intentions based on some kind of character flaw.

In psychology, this is known as the "fundamental attribution error", which is the tendency for people to overemphasise personality-based explanations for other people's behaviours and to overemphasise situational factors when it comes to their own actions (Ross, 1977). Sometimes they may be correct and the villain is deliberately setting out to harm them, but there are other times when something else is the cause and the client simply does not have all of the necessary information.

Let me give you a personal example. I have a friend who is notoriously always late. I, on the other hand, am always early! So, whenever my friend and I arranged to do something together, I was doomed to be frustrated, because I always ended up waiting for her. On this particular day, we had arranged to see a movie together. I was early so bought both our tickets and waited for her to arrive. The movie was about to start and she still wasn't there. I tried calling her on her mobile but it was engaged. Now, this wasn't an unusual situation. She often got caught up having a chat to someone on the phone and lost track of time. As I waited and waited, the movie had already started and my friend was still not there. I tried to call a few times and each time the phone was engaged. In my mind I could see her, sitting in her car in the carpark, chatting away, not realising the time. I decided that enough was enough. This was my moment to be assertive and deal with the situation. Eventually she answered the phone. Before she could even get a word in, I launched into my assertive speech. "The movie has already started, and I've bought both our tickets. I'm so sick of you being late all the time. It shows a lack of respect for me and our friendship. Why couldn't you at least message me? Where are you?" There was a long pause and then a little voice at the end of the phone said, "I'm sorry, I was talking to Mum. ... Dad just died ...". That was a fairly important piece of information that I wished I had before launching into my assertive conflict speech. I would have had quite a different conversation had I known that at the start, but I didn't even give her a chance to tell me. I just assumed that she was late for no good reason, because it was a character flaw.

Here's an equally awful example from a mediation I conducted a few years ago. Two women in a workplace were in the middle of a highly escalated conflict. One of the women, Betty, was convinced (she was *certain*) that the other woman, Sue, was deliberately undermining her. According to Betty, the conflict started when Sue began asking Betty to put everything they discussed at work in writing. Betty would ask Sue to do something, and Sue would say to Betty, "Can you please write that down for me?" or "Can you please put that in an email to me?" Betty became very suspicious about Sue's intentions. She couldn't understand why a simple request had to be put in writing. She developed a story in her mind that Sue was compiling a dossier of material to use against Betty for some nasty reason. Things became very tense between them. When I was called in to mediate, the two women could barely even look at each other. As the discussion started, Betty exploded. She became highly emotional and accused Sue of all sorts of horrible things and kept referring to her "file" of things that she was collecting against her. Sue asked Betty what she meant by the file. Betty said that it was all the things that Sue had required her to put in writing for no good reason and said words to the effect that it was completely ridiculous what Sue needed in writing. Sue was quiet for a long time. Then she said with a wavering voice, "I didn't want to have to tell people this, I had hoped that I could continue working without people noticing, but I guess it's time to explain. You see, I have a brain tumour. It's getting worse, and it's affecting my short-term memory. I need things to be written down for me, or I forget them. I didn't want to tell people because I didn't want to be forced to go on sick leave – I really need to keep working." You can imagine the impact that new piece of information had on the conflict and how Betty felt about things.

When working with clients in conflict, the coach should look out for times that the client is making assumptions about another person's intentions. These are usually not difficult to identify in a melodramatic conflict story. Here's a common example that I see come up for many of my clients. Gerald reported to me that he was becoming more and more frustrated with his colleague Harriet's behaviour. They both worked in an open plan workspace, and Harriet's and Gerald's desks were next to each other. Gerald explained that Harriet was constantly interfering in his work, leaning over and making suggestions about what Gerald should be doing. It was driving Gerald crazy! In Gerald's words, "She obviously thinks that I'm not capable of doing my job on my own, because she's always telling me what to do. If I need help, I'll ask someone for it. I wish she'd just mind her own business." Gerald was certain that Harriet's behaviour was driven by her belief that he was incompetent. Though this might have been true, it was important to explore this further to identify any uncertainty. I asked Gerald what it was about Harriet's behaviour that made him believe that she thought he was incompetent. His answer was, effectively, that "it was obvious". I persevered, asking him what it was that made it obvious. Gerald explained that he had never asked Harriet for her help and that she persisted in interrupting him and interfering, so "what other reason could there be?" I redirected the question back to Gerald, asking him "What other reason *could* there be for Harriet's behaviour?" He looked a bit confused by the question but then started to come up with some other possibilities. He said, "Well, I guess she might think that she is just being helpful, but it's bloody annoying!" I asked him what might indicate that Harriet thinks she's being helpful. Gerald replied that the fact that she kept on doing it, even though he found it extremely irritating, suggested that she thought she was being helpful. I asked Gerald to imagine that I was talking to Harriet and that I asked her why she was behaving in this way and what he thought Harriet might reply. His immediate response was that he wasn't sure.

This uncertainty was a significant positive step, because at this point we could start to have a conversation about how he might find out more about what was driving Harriet's behaviour. Gerald had started to shift from certainty to uncertainty and towards curiosity. I asked him how he might find out more about what Harriet's intention was, and he realised that he had never actually asked her! Nor, he conceded, had he ever specifically told her how annoying he found her behaviour – he just assumed that she should know this! This is another area of uncertainty that the coach should explore with clients in conflict: the impact of their actions on others.

Develop uncertainty about intent and impact

As well as typically assuming that the "villain" does everything with an evil intention, clients in conflict frequently present themselves as only having good intentions, and they also assume that the impact of their actions on others is consistent with these good intentions when performing that action. However, a client can rarely be completely certain about the impact of their behaviour.

Let's consider Gerald's conflict from Harriet's perspective. If I were coaching Harriet and I asked her about her working relationship with Gerald, she might say something like, "Oh, it's fine. I like to keep an eye on him and help him out every now and then." I could then invite her to describe how she helps Gerald out and how she perceives his reaction. It is likely that she would describe Gerald as finding her interventions helpful, because this is how she intends them. However, I would then ask her to consider some other ways that Gerald might perceive her "helpfulness" in an attempt to create some uncertainty about her assumptions. Depending on how open she was to considering other possibilities, I might ask more directly, "In what ways might Gerald find your interactions unhelpful?"

Identify other uncertainties and unknowns

The coach should be aware of opportunities to highlight uncertainty and unknowns in the client's story. There are certain phrases that clients use that typically signal uncertainty or unknowns, including:

- I think that …
- I'm not sure …
- I don't know …
- I guess maybe …
- I have no idea …
- Probably/possibly …

The coach should look for opportunities to ask questions about what is unknown or uncertain in the client's story. In asking questions about these areas of the client's story, the aim is not to develop knowledge or certainty; rather, it's about supporting the client to acknowledge what they don't know for sure and explore whether it's important for them to find out and, if so, how they might do that.

Some useful questions include:

- What would happen if you are wrong about that (assumption)?
- What makes you think that?
- What information do you have that supports that as the most likely conclusion?
- What could you be missing here?
- What difference would it make if you were 100 percent sure about that?
- How could you find out?
- What are some other possible explanations for [the other's] actions?

Developing uncertainty about the right outcome

Clients stuck in a melodramatic conflict story are usually certain about how the problem should be resolved: the villain should receive their comeuppance and the protagonist should be restored to their position of virtue as it was prior to the villain's interference. However, as we will discuss in more detail in Chapter 14, the past is usually not as ideal as the client portrays it, and the notion of "dream justice" is either unrealistic or likely to come at a cost. It is important to support clients to develop a sense of uncertainty about the right outcome, so that they are motivated to reality test a number of alternatives and to work towards improving their future choices.

In George's case (discussed in Chapter 8), coaching helped him identify that though "dream justice" may be available, in the sense that he had a strong legal case of discrimination against his current employer, there were downsides to that outcome that made him choose not to pursue it. Similarly, Angela, early in our coaching session, decided that if there was no way she could make Georgia resign, then she would confront her about her behaviour and warn her that Angela would file a bullying complaint against her if she didn't stop making Angela's life a misery. Though in one sense this was progress from Angela just sitting around complaining and waiting for someone to save her, in that she was now considering doing something active herself to resolve her suffering, it was not necessarily the best choice Angela could make.

When clients come up with an action plan – *any* action plan – this can often seem like significant progress for them and they can begin to focus on that plan to the exclusion of further exploration of other options. It is important for the coach to slow the client down and encourage them to explore further before committing to the first option they come up with. Reality testing is a useful tool to develop uncertainty about the client's idea of the right outcome. Asking questions about the best- and worst-case scenarios and things that might get in the way of that outcome working as planned can be very helpful.

It's also useful for the coach to ask questions that imply that there may even be another, better option. Sometimes simply assuming this can prompt a client to develop a better "plan B". Without entirely dismissing a client's action plan, a coach can acknowledge that the client's plan is certainly one option and then encourage them to consider other different (and perhaps better) options. The coach can continuously reinforce the fact that, for the moment at least, their options are still open, and it might be worth considering other alternatives before entirely committing to one action.

Conclusion

Developing a sense of uncertainty is helpful in managing conflict because, firstly, it is more realistic – we never know everything there is to know about what is going on – and secondly, because it leads to curiosity and a more open mind. This shift has its foundations in the first shift (from simplicity to complexity) and then leads to the third shift (from passive to active), because as people become curious and realise that there are multiple possibilities for the future, they are also likely to be more open to taking steps towards finding out information that might help them become more certain and improve their situation.

REFERENCE

Ross, L. 1977. The intuitive psychologist and his shortcomings: distortions in the attribution process. In Berkowitz, L. (Ed.), *Advances in experimental social psychology*, Vol. 10, pp. 173–220. New York: Academic Press.

12

PASSIVE TO ACTIVE

Clients who have cast themselves as the victim in a melodramatic conflict story tend to present as helplessly passive characters, with other people acting upon them. However, a close analysis of their stories will frequently reveal instances where the client has self-initiated action or has had an opportunity to act but has chosen not to do so (for various reasons). The coach's role is to assist the client to identify those instances and to recognise that passivity is frequently a choice, not a foregone conclusion.

The coach should support clients to recognise that, despite having presented themselves in a quite passive and helpless role, they have inevitably made choices about their behaviour so far in this situation, and they also have choices about what to do in the future. Sometimes these choices may not be ideal (the choice may be between one bad option and one worse option) but the client still has some input into which of these choices they take. Helping a client recognise choices can be a significant step towards a feeling of self-determination and agency.

DOI: 10.4324/9781003128038-12

Identify and evaluate past choices (good and bad)

The first step in making the shift from passive to active is to help the client identify choices they have made in the past, both good and bad. Clients generally do not describe past choices as if they have had agency; rather, they describe situations as if someone else (usually the villain) has forced them to do something. For example, in Angela's conflict story Angela talks about a situation during her induction when Georgia said something to her like, "Is this okay for you or do you want my desk and chair?" Angela explains that though she had all these smart replies in her head and normally she "would have given it back to her", at that moment she was "tongue-tied". She presents the situation as if somehow Georgia was not letting her say what she wanted to say in return, that she had no choice but to remain silent. However, in that moment, Angela was not actually forced into silence. Rather, she made a choice not to reply.

I did not directly point this out to Angela, because this may have made her feel judged and defensive. Instead, I implied that she had made a choice when asking her to tell me more about the incident. I asked a question that included the fact that she had made a choice in the wording of the question. I said, "Angela, at that moment when Georgia said those things to you and you had all these smart replies in your head, you chose not to say any of them. What was it that made you choose that response?" Angela responded by saying, "Oh, well, you just can't say those kinds of things to a work colleague, especially on your first day!" I then highlighted to Angela that she had, in fact, made a wise choice in the circumstances, saying something like, "So it sounds like in that moment, by not saying the things that you were thinking, you made a really smart choice not to say what you really wanted to say!"

I then asked Angela to tell me what she would have liked to have said if there were no consequences: "Angela, if you could have said anything you wanted to at that moment, what would you have liked to have said?" Angela replied with something like, "I would have said, 'Georgia, you're such a bitch, how dare you say that to me on my first day. What kind of person are you?'" Clients often really like it when the coach gives them the opportunity to let go of their virtue and say something really inappropriate out loud. They often say those things with some relish and laugh about it. When the client laughs, this also opens up a learning opportunity. I usually ask the client, "Why is it funny when you say that?" And they say, "Oh, because I would never say that, that's really inappropriate. You don't use language like that or speak to people like that in the workplace". And again, I can highlight for the client the fact that they've made a smart choice not to say what they really wanted to say in that moment.

The fact that the client made a good choice not to say something highly inappropriate does not mean, however, that there might not have been some other choices available to them that were better than saying nothing. In Angela's case, we have now confirmed that there were choices available to her in that moment and that out of the two we have discussed, one (saying nothing) was better than the other (being rude). We have also then opened up the possibility that there were other choices available to Angela in that moment. We can now ask Angela whether, in hindsight, there were other things that she could have chosen to say to manage the situation better. We support the client in learning by self-reflection. And though the client cannot go back and re-do that conversation, the client is expanding their repertoire of possible responses in the future, should they face a similar situation. They are learning to identify and evaluate multiple choices using this situation as an example, and when they move into the future planning stage of this process, they are much more likely to identify a variety of choices for future action.

Clients who are stuck in a melodramatic conflict story can struggle to recognise that they have made any choices that may have led to the conflict arising, persisting, or escalating. Using Claire's story about her conflict with Alison, her flatmate, as an example, we see very little information in her version of events about her possible contributions to the conflict arising. She doesn't tell us what information she provided to Alison about her expectations about sharing food when Alison first moved in. She doesn't tell us about any conversations she may have had with Alison about this since Alison moved in or when Claire noticed her using Claire's food. The story implies that Claire hasn't said anything, but this may not be the case. It seems possible that Claire has contributed to this conflict with Alison in a number of ways; for example, by not being clear about her expectations about food sharing when Alison first moved in and by not raising her concerns explicitly when Alison started using her food without asking. Exploring Claire's contribution to the conflict may be useful to her (if a little uncomfortable at the time) because it may open up ideas for her to contribute to better managing the situation (now with Alison and in the future with other flatmates). Some of this information may come up as we ask Claire to provide more details about what has been happening with Alison. However, we can also ask some more direct questions about Claire's actions (or inactions) in the past. For example, we could ask Claire, "What conversations did you have with Alison prior to her moving in with you?" and "What did you say to Alison when you first noticed her using your food without asking?" We could also ask questions such as, "In hindsight, what could you have done to prevent this conflict occurring?" and "What would you do next time, with a new flatmate, to ensure that this kind of situation did not happen again?"

Even when the client's past choices have not contributed to the conflict arising, it is usually the case that the client has made choices that have at least created the context for the conflict to arise. Recognising these choices is not in itself likely to provide a solution to the conflict. However, it does provide a reminder to the client that they have made choices in the past and that they have capacity to make choices in the future. Though we can't necessarily create the ideal kind of choices the client wishes existed, we can continually highlight their capacity to have some control over their future, irrespective of the challenges they currently face.

Adrian's story is a good example of how clients can be supported to recognise their capacity to identify and make choices, even in difficult circumstances. Adrian was a PhD candidate who was having a very difficult time with his doctoral supervisor. He reported that his supervisor was constantly undermining him and using him as a technical assistant to produce data for his (the supervisor's) own purposes, rather than supporting Adrian to complete his PhD. He said that his supervisor kept requiring him to do certain experiments that in Adrian's opinion were not relevant for his PhD topic. He also said that his supervisor frequently presented Adrian's data and analysis at conferences without acknowledging that it was Adrian's work. He said when he tried to organise supervision meetings with his supervisor, the supervisor was frequently "too busy", and then when his supervisor did meet with Adrian he was highly critical and negative about anything Adrian had produced. Adrian said this had been happening for over a year, and with less than 18 months left to complete his thesis, Adrian was starting to feel very stressed and anxious. Adrian was holding on to a desperate hope that someone would be able to make his supervisor change his behaviour, so that

Adrian could successfully complete his PhD. So far, nobody had come to his rescue. The Graduate Research School staff suggested that he either "tough it out" or try to find another supervisor, but neither of these things seemed possible to Adrian: he felt unable to continue with his studies the way things were going with his current supervisor and found it difficult to even turn up to the university. He had also made enquiries about other potential supervisors, but nobody in his university had the relevant expertise. He felt completely stuck and that he had no control or choices in the situation.

However, if we look at Adrian's situation closely, there were a number of choices he had made leading up to this conflict situation. Some of them may have been good choices, and some of them may not have been the best choice in the circumstances. However, the fact is that Adrian had made choices and taken (or at least tried to take) control of aspects of the situation.

Adrian's past choices included choosing to do a PhD, choosing to do it at this university, choosing to do it with this particular supervisor, choosing to do the experiments his supervisor required even when he thought they were not relevant, choosing not to talk directly with his supervisor about his concerns, approaching the Graduate Research School for advice, choosing to make enquiries about other supervisors, choosing not to give up his studies, choosing not to go in to the university unless absolutely necessary, and choosing to come to see a conflict coach for support. None of these choices are necessarily good or bad in the circumstances, but they do demonstrate some agency, despite the challenging and seemingly unfair situation that Adrian found himself.

Identify future choices

Adrian also had a number of choices about what to do next, although many of them did not seem particularly attractive to him at the time. He did not feel like he had many choices, but once we started discussing different possibilities, and variations on each of those, he began to see that he actually had many choices available to him (even though none of them were ideal). Adrian identified the following choices: deferring his PhD studies, quitting his PhD (just dropping it altogether or trying to exit with a MPhil instead), or continuing with his PhD studies (either at this university with this supervisor or at another university with another supervisor). Adrian identified some choices within those choices. If he stayed with his current supervisor, he could choose to do nothing further to try to resolve the problem and just "tough it out" or he could try to find a co-supervisor to support him. He realised that if he were to continue in this way, he could also seek support from a coach or counsellor to better manage the situation without confronting the supervisor. Alternatively, Adrian could confront his current supervisor with his concerns and/or make a formal complaint about his supervisor through the university complaints process. Though none of these options were ideal from Adrian's perspective, at least he felt like he now had some control of how he managed a very difficult situation.

Sometimes clients do not realise that a choice is available to them that might significantly improve their future. Beverly's story is good example. Beverly was the founder of a charitable organisation that had developed over the years into quite a large and well-respected body. When the organisation started, it was largely a one-person enterprise, with Beverly doing everything. As the organisation developed, more people became involved and a more formal framework was established. Beverly was the founding president of the board of directors, a role she had held for almost ten years. Beverly was starting to make the transition into retirement and felt that it was now time for her to start stepping back from the organisation and allowing someone younger with some fresh ideas to take over the president role. She announced her resignation from the role of president (but her intention to remain a board member) and a new president was elected.

In the subsequent months, Beverly explained that she had significant difficulties in her relationship with the new president. She felt that, at every board meeting, the new president was explicitly undermining her contributions to any discussion and that the new president's behaviour towards her was outright rude. Beverly spent a great deal of time explaining how stressed and upset she had become as a result of the new president's behaviour at these board meetings and what an impact the situation was having on her entire life. Beverly became quite emotional as she was talking about this, and as she collected herself I said to her, "Wow, it sounds like those board meetings are really horrible and they are causing you significant stress. What's making you keep going to them?" Beverly was dumbfounded by the question and couldn't answer it. She said she would have to think about it for a few days and would tell me her answer in our next coaching session.

In the next session, she arrived a different woman and excitedly informed me that she had resigned from the board altogether. Though she was a little disappointed at having to leave her role on the board, she had recognised that it was the right thing for her, and possibly also for the organisation. She was so relieved that she didn't have to suffer through the board meetings any more. She was quite amazed at the power of that one question I had asked in the previous session. She explained that it had not even occurred to her that she had the choice to remove herself from the situation.

Beverly, in one sense, was lucky in that she did have the ability to resign from the board at that time. For some employees, leaving their job is not always an option. However, even for people who might be somewhat "stuck" in a conflict situation, there are frequently things that they could do to alleviate their suffering to some extent. Note that actions taken to alleviate suffering, or to minimise the negative impacts of the conflict, are different from actions taken to resolve the conflict. In Beverly's situation, the things that she could potentially do to alleviate her suffering would not necessarily address her conflict with the villain of her story.

Turning uncertainty into action

As clients develop uncertainty about their conflict story, this also opens up opportunities for action. When a client recognises that there is something they do not know, or something that they do not fully understand, they can passively accept this or they can choose to do something about it. They can gather information, ask questions, try to find out whatever it is that is missing from their story that might be helpful to them in deciding how to manage it in the future. For example, in Kevin's situation (Chapter 3), as we talked through his conflict with Bill, his new team leader, he realised that he wasn't really sure about why Bill was behaving so negatively towards him. He assumed that it was because Bill was just "a jerk", but he did acknowledge that there may be something else going on for Bill that Kevin didn't know about. Kevin explored ways that he might find out more about what was driving Bill's behaviour, including things like directly asking him, observing Bill more closely, trying some different ways to interact with him, and consulting some colleagues. He also recognised that, though he was nervous about talking to his manager about the situation, he was not entirely sure how his manager might respond. He acknowledged that one consequence of speaking with his manager might be that his manager could perceive that Kevin did not get along with his colleagues, but he also admitted that there were other possible outcomes, including that his manager might be impressed with Kevin making an effort to address the situation in a proactive way. We also explored other possible actions that Kevin could take, other than speaking directly with Bill and/or his manager. Kevin identified that he thought there were other processes available to him within the organisation. There was some kind of formal grievance process (which he agreed to find out more about) and there was some other confidential counselling through the Employee Assistance Scheme that he could access for free that he acknowledged might be useful. He also thought that there might be people in human resources whom he could discuss his situation with on an informal and confidential basis. All of these ideas gave Kevin a range of positive steps he could take to find out more about his options. Though there was no guarantee that any of these steps would lead to the resolution of his conflict with Bill, the fact that he was actively doing something to try to find the best way forward gave Kevin a new sense of purpose and control over his own life.

Conclusion

The shift from passive to active is an important one, both psychologically (because it gives the client a sense of control over their own destiny, which is important for resilience and well-being) and practically (because the client develops positive steps that they can take to improve their situation). One of the fundamental problems with the melodramatic protagonist role is that they have to sit around, suffering, while waiting for someone to rescue them. Once a client identifies that they do have options for action, they develop a sense of purpose and become proactive, which almost inevitably does lead to some improvement in their situation, if not a fully resolved conflict.

13

DEPENDENCE TO AGENCY

In the melodramatic conflict narrative, the protagonist is dependent on others to recognise their virtue and dispense dream justice. However, in the tragic conflict narrative, the protagonist becomes a hero, taking matters into their own hands and making positive steps to improve their situation as much as they can in the circumstances. Tragic heroes are independent and resilient and develop the skills to manage their own challenges where possible.

There are a number of things we can do as coach to support a client to make the move away from dependence to agency. The first is to get the client engaged in taking responsibility right from the start of the coaching process. The most obvious way to do this is to ask the client to set a goal for the coaching conversation, rather than leaving it up to the coach or others to direct the client about what would be helpful to work on. The coach should also always encourage the client to make their own decisions during the coaching by asking the client to make choices throughout the session wherever possible. The coach should also invite the client to do

DOI: 10.4324/9781003128038-13

things themselves during the coaching session, rather than doing things for them. For example, the coach can ask the client to summarise what they have spoken about so far, rather than summarising back to them. The coach should also avoid giving advice or suggestions and consistently encourage the client to come up with their own ideas. Finally, the coach can encourage the client to "play" with agency, by giving them a safe space to experiment with various actions they may choose to take in the future.

Encourage the client to take responsibility right from the start

It is important that clients take responsibility for their engagement in the coaching process. One way to encourage clients to take responsibility right from the start it to ask them to identify goals that they want to achieve by participating in coaching (or something similar). One of the reasons that goal setting is so useful at the start of a coaching session (even when the goal is more than likely to change during a session) is that it prompts the client to take responsibility for what they want to achieve in the session right from the outset. It highlights to the client that the coach is there to support the client to work towards what the client wants to achieve, not what the coach thinks the client should be doing.

There are a couple of things to keep in mind for coaches when supporting someone in developing a goal in the beginning of a coaching session. Firstly, clients in conflict are usually very good at telling us what they do not want but not as good at explaining what they do want. As a coach, we need to support the client to come up with a positive goal, something they can work towards (not run away from). When a client uses language like, "I want this to stop" or "I don't want to feel like this", we should ask them to reframe this into something that they can actively work towards – for example, questions like, "What would you like to be happening instead?" or "How would you like to be feeling instead?" This is another situation when our special listening skills are important. We need to listen to the kind of language that a client uses when they explain what they hope to achieve in coaching.

Similarly, clients often frame an initial goal as making someone else change (usually the villain in their conflict story). The coach should refocus the client towards something that the client has agency to change (i.e., themselves). Questions that can be useful here include "How possible do you think it is for you to change X's behaviour?" or "What kinds of things do you think you could do to motivate X to change their behaviour?" If the client is stuck in a melodramatic conflict story, they are likely to respond to those questions in a helpless way, indicating that they don't feel able to effect those changes. Though this can be a bit of a disheartening start, the coach can then refocus the client on what the client *does* have agency over. "If X changed in that way, what would be different for you?" and then "Would you like to explore some ways you might be able to work towards those differences yourself?"

Clients also sometimes present their goal as something they think they *should* be working towards (because someone else has told them this or there is some external pressure on them to achieve it). For a client to truly have agency, they need to have a very clear idea of their own personal needs and aspirations, so that they are truly motivated to take appropriate action. Clients will never fully engage with a goal that they do not genuinely believe in. The coach should encourage and support the client in identifying what they truly need and to develop some action steps towards meeting those needs.

Peter came to me as a coaching client at the request of his manager Cheryl. Peter's organisation was paying for his coaching sessions as part of his professional development program. When I spoke with Peter about what he hoped to achieve from participating in coaching, he informed me that Cheryl had given him feedback during his last performance management session that he needed to be less friendly with his team and become a stronger leader. Peter said that this was what he wanted to work on in our coaching sessions. Though this did seem like a goal that Peter *could* work on during coaching, I wondered how invested he was in achieving what Cheryl had suggested. I asked Peter how he felt about potentially becoming less friendly with his team and turning into what Cheryl saw as a stronger leader. As he spoke, it became clear that he was not entirely on board with the idea but that he felt that he should do what Cheryl asked because it was important to keep his manager happy. Though I do not, as a coach, routinely encourage clients to go against their managers' directions, I do often encourage clients to explore how their managers' wishes might be more or less consistent with their own needs and values. When a client tries to work on a goal that they do not really believe in, a number of things are likely to happen. Firstly, they may struggle to achieve the goal because they are not motivated to put in the effort to do so. Secondly, if they do achieve the goal, they can end up resentful, and this can lead to other problems in their relationships or their general well-being in the future.

An important part of developing a client's agency is encouraging them to critically analyse requests from other people for them to change something about themselves. This is not the same thing as automatically being resistant to someone else's feedback. Rather, it is about consciously reviewing the feedback in light of the client's own needs and values and thinking realistically about the consequences of working towards any change, before taking any steps to do so.

Encourage the client to make decisions during the coaching session

The coach should demonstrate whereever possible that the client has agency during the coaching session. This includes always giving the client choice about what they want to talk about and even allowing them the choice to not talk about something. For example, when the client talks about two different things that could potentially be discussed in more detail, saying something to the client like, "You've talked about X and Y. Which of these things would you like to focus on?" Similarly, when the client's train of thought finishes and they stop talking and look to the coach for input, asking, "Would you like to say more about that, or would you prefer to move on to talking about something else now?"

There are often times in a coaching session during which the coach wonders what to say next, which question to ask, or whether it's time to move into a new stage of the process. These are also opportunities to support the client in developing agency. A simple check-in can be a useful strategy in those moments. Saying things like, "What are your thoughts about our conversation so far?" and "What do you think might be helpful to explore next?" both encourage the client to engage in self-reflection and make a choice about what direction they'd like to take the conversation next. Rather than waiting for someone else to tell them what they should think or do, you are giving them the opportunity to make their own choice in the moment.

Invite the client to do things themselves

If you have previously been trained as a mediator, or done courses on active listening, you will be inclined to want to paraphrase and summarise what clients say. However, in coaching this is less important and can sometimes result in the client becoming dependent on you to help them clarify and sort their thoughts and experiences. Whenever possible, the coach should invite the client to do these things themselves. Statements such as, "Remind me what the main events were leading up to the big argument", "summarise for me the things that matter to you most in this situation", and "remind me what you are going to do after this session" are helpful ways to remind the client that they have control and are empowered to determine their own future.

There are also moments in coaching where a client may consider action steps that involve asking someone else to do something that they could potentially do themselves. The coach should be aware of those moments and take the opportunity to supportively challenge the client about the benefits and risks of handing over their agency to someone else. A common example that arises in workplace conflicts is when a client has a conflict with a colleague's behaviour and, instead of speaking with the colleague directly about their concerns, decides to speak with a manager and try to have the manager approach the colleague on their behalf. Penny's conflict with her colleague Nicolas is a good illustration of this type of situation.

Penny was growing more and more irritated at Nicolas's behaviour at work. She complained that he took longer breaks for morning tea, lunch, and afternoon tea than the other team members and that he took additional breaks in between these times to go and have a cigarette out the back of the building. During the times that he was away from his desk, Penny had to take his calls and manage any enquiries that came in for Nicolas. When considering her choices for how to respond to this situation, Penny suggested that she talk to their team leader, Francis, and ask her to tell Nicolas that he can't keep taking these breaks and expecting other team members to cover him. Though in one sense it was her team leader's responsibility to manage the time of team members and monitor their breaks, there were also potential risks in Penny choosing this option rather than speaking directly to Nicolas (or at least attempting to speak to Nicolas first). I asked Penny to imagine that Francis agreed to speak with Nicholas about his breaks. I asked her what she thought Francis might say to him. I asked her to consider some variations in what Francis might say. I asked her to think about any unintended consequences that might arise from Francis speaking to Nicolas at Penny's request. At first Penny could not imagine any but she soon identified that there was a risk that Francis might tell Nicolas that it was Penny who had complained about him and that this could lead to Francis developing a grudge against Penny and make it difficult for them to work together. She also acknowledged that even if Francis did not name Penny, Nicolas would probably guess that it was she who had complained, because it was obvious that Penny was the one who had the greatest load in covering for Nicolas when he was away from his desk.

I also asked Penny to imagine a situation in which one of her colleagues had a problem with something she was doing at work. Would she prefer them to go directly to Francis to complain or would she prefer they do something else? Penny began to realise that though getting Francis to approach Nicolas seemed like an easier option, it might create different problems between Penny and Nicolas in the future. She also identified that Francis may be annoyed at having to deal with this on Penny's behalf and that could affected their relationship in the future. Penny realised that although there were benefits in having someone else speak to Nicolas on her behalf, it meant that she had less control over what was said and the aftermath of those conversations. Though talking directly to him was more difficult, it did mean that she had some control over what was said and how it was raised with him.

Don't give advice or suggestions

In the example above with Penny, I was careful not to directly say to her, "Hey, Penny, don't you think it would be better to talk directly with Nicolas yourself, rather than getting Francis to do it?" Rather, I asked her some general questions about the potential benefits and risks of complaining to Francis rather than Nicolas directly and let Penny figure out for herself which option was likely to be best for her. In doing so, I was attempting to support Penny's agency to figure out things herself and make her own smart choices. I wasn't leaving her entirely unsupported but was keeping my support to the bare minimum to encourage her to think a bit more carefully about her choices.

When a client asks you directly what you think about their situation or what you think they should do, redirect the question back to your client. For example, "It's more important for you to be clear about what *you* think about your situation and what *you* think you should do, because you are the one who is going to have to do it, not me! Tell me what you are thinking about your situation right now. What are the areas that seem unclear or most difficult to you right now?" Depending on the level of rapport and trust between coach and client, the coach could even draw the client's attention to their need for advice or direction. For example, when the client asks the coach what they should do, the coach could respond with "I'm wondering how you think my advice would be helpful to you?" This question can sometimes lead to a client reflecting about whether they really do need advice from someone (in which case the coach can help them identify more appropriate people to provide that advice to them) or whether they are simply looking for an easy way out of having to do the work of figuring it out for themselves.

Another useful strategy when a client asks the coach for advice is to invite the client to identify other people whom the client respects and to ask the client to imagine what advice they might give the client in this situation. For example, when the client asks the coach for advice, the coach says something like, "I'm probably not the best person to give you advice here. Who else can you think of who is likely to be able to give you wise advice about this situation?" The client may identify person X. The coach can then ask the client, "If person X were here now, and you asked them what they would suggest, what do you think they would say to you?" Sometimes this question can prompt the client to come up with different ideas simply by putting themselves in another person's shoes, so to speak, in that moment.

As discussed in the previous chapter, when a situation or a choice is a difficult one, having someone tell us what to do saves us the effort of having to think it through and make that choice ourselves. It seems easier, but it's usually less effective. Others do not have the same depth of understanding of our own needs and concerns, and others do not have to face the consequences of our actions.

Give the client opportunities to 'play' with agency

Sometimes the reality is that the client does have agency but they are afraid to use it. In a coaching session we can give the client an opportunity to play with their potential agency in a safe space, to see how it feels and to explore the kind of impact that enacting it might have.

For example, Peter expressed his lack of agency in the way he talked about his manager Cheryl and her control over his future employment (through performance management, etc.). He explained that he "had to" do what she wanted him to do about his leadership style to avoid a negative performance appraisal or other consequences. In a coaching session, I can give Peter the opportunity to explore what agency might feel like if those perceived constraints were not present. I could, for example, invite Peter to imagine that he had a different manager who fully supported Peter developing his own style of leadership. I could ask Peter to explain how he would interact with and lead his team and why he would make those choices. I could ask him to explore how his style of leadership would affect his team, his manager, and the broader organisation. Though in Peter's current reality this may not be possible (or at least not possible if Cheryl insisted that Peter adopt a different approach), imagining it in detail in a coaching session may have some positive effects on Peter and his perception of his choices and their consequences. Peter might develop some arguments in favour of his way of leading his team that he could discuss with Cheryl if the topic came up again. He may reach an understanding that his values and beliefs about leadership are quite different from Cheryl's and that he was not going to be supported in leading in his own way while Cheryl was his manager. This could result in Peter looking for other roles within or outside the organisation in which his leadership style was supported. Another possibility is that Peter identifies that there are some shortcomings in his perspective about how effective leaders interact with their team and is motivated to adapt his behaviour in some way (which may address some of Cheryl's concerns). Even if Peter decides that he will take Cheryl's feedback on board and change his behaviour in accordance with her wishes, by having gone through this kind of process at least he will recognise that, though he doesn't necessarily like this choice, he is making it willingly because the benefits to him of doing so outweigh the risks of not complying. He is making a choice to do what Cheryl asks and not simply following directions because he feels that he has to do so.

Conclusion

The most important thing to keep in mind when coaching someone in conflict is that you want to provide them with opportunities to become empowered, both now and into the future. Your aim is to provide just enough support so that they think more carefully about the possibilities for action (and inaction) before choosing what to do. You also want to help them learn how to be independent and manage conflict themselves into the future, as far as it is safe for them to do so. You want to discourage them from simply first taking the easy way forward and encourage them to look for ways to develop more agency and control over their own future. This is like the old saying about giving a person a fish: we don't want to just give them a fish, we want to teach them *how to fish* so that they will not be dependent on others having to feed them in the future.

SOME USEFUL QUESTIONS FOR HELPING PEOPLE SHIFT FROM DEPENDENCY TO AGENCY

What do *you* want?

How do *you* feel about that?

If you didn't have to worry about what other people thought, what would you say/do?

What choice do you really want to make here?

What's most important to *you*?

If your partner/best friend was in your situation, what would you advise them to do and why?

14

PAST TO FUTURE

In melodramatic stories, the appropriate resolution of the conflict is a return to the status quo. This entails a focus on the past and assumes that the way things *should be* is the way things *have been*, thus limiting consideration of the way things could be different and even improved (Hardy, 2008). It is possible to coach someone using a solution-focused approach, in which the client does not even consider the past and starts from the present looking forward. However, this can result in the client building a future action plan based on an incomplete understanding, or misunderstanding, of the past. Accordingly, I recommend that, when time permits, the client be supported to reflect and learn from the past aspect of their story before developing a future action plan. There is, however, a time in the coaching process when the client needs to be encouraged to let go of the past and look forward towards the future. Though we want our clients to learn from the past, we do not want them to hold on to it, constantly looking backwards. We want them to be future-focused.

DOI: 10.4324/9781003128038-14

There are a number of ways to support the client's shift from past to future. The first is to encourage a realistic view of the past. The second is to support the client to realise that it is not possible to return to the past because inevitably things have changed as a result of the conflict. The third is to help the client to recognise that they can do better than return to the past – that they can improve the future. Finally, the coach can encourage the client to take the opportunity to actively create their own future.

Encourage a realistic view of the past

Remember Claire's conflict with her flatmate Alison (Chapter 3)? Claire begins her conflict story by describing the ideal situation she used to have with her previous flatmate Emma. Claire describes a relationship in which it was like "living with a sister or my best friend" and explains that she never minded sharing food or her car with Emma because Emma always made up for it in some way. Claire acknowledges that she probably replaced things more often than Emma but she felt that was fair because she earnt more money than Emma.

Though it probably is true that Claire's experience of sharing with Emma was better than her current experience sharing with Alison, there could be many reasons for the difference (other than Alison being a horrible person). It is also likely that there were moments when Claire was sharing with Emma that were not perfect and that Claire either ignored or managed and resolved these situations at the time. The following example demonstrates how identifying and discussing examples of things that were not ideal in the past gave Claire ideas and confidence that there may be ways to improve the things that were currently not ideal with Alison.

When I asked Claire to talk more about what it was like sharing with Emma, she provided lots of positive examples. I then asked her to tell me about a time when she found living with Emma a challenge. Claire thought about this for a moment and then described a time when Emma was dating someone who used to stay over a couple of times a week and how Claire found it awkward to have Emma's boyfriend in the apartment. I asked her to describe what was awkward about having him there, and she mentioned lack of privacy (she didn't feel comfortable walking from the bathroom to her room wearing just her underwear, which she would normally do if it was just Emma home) and that "Steve used to eat everything in the fridge!"

I asked Claire to describe how she managed that situation at the time, and she told me that she spoke with Emma about it one evening when Steve wasn't there, and though Emma insisted that her boyfriend be able to stay over any time he wanted to, she did make sure that he started to bring food with him or ordered pizza delivery for all of them if he was going to be there for dinner.

Though exploring some of the challenges during Claire's past flatmate experience does not directly help her current challenges with Alison, it does provide her with a bit of perspective on the situation. When the past is not so "idealised", the future sometimes does not seem so bad. When Claire thinks about how she managed past challenges, she also begins to think about how she might apply some of those strategies to her current situation.

Similarly, in many workplace conflicts, clients idealise the past and the opportunities they felt were available to them that were subsequently "stolen" by the villain. For example, Kevin describes his experience at work before Bill was appointed to the team leader role as being unproblematic (Chapter 3). He says he was well-respected by his colleagues, his work was seen as excellent, his performance reviews were always positive, and that everyone was happy and productive. Kevin explains that to his (and everyone's) surprise, he didn't get the team leader role. In effect, he implies that Bill stole the role that was rightfully Kevin's. There is room here to explore the reality of Kevin's view of the past, particularly his expectation of obtaining the team leader role. It may be that there are some good reasons why Kevin was not appointed to the role that have nothing to do with Bill. This information may be useful to Kevin in the future, if he can explore the past with a little less idealism. In coaching, I asked Kevin to talk to me about his expectations of getting the team leader role. I invited him to share with me what the application process involved and what made him feel so certain that he would be appointed. I also asked him some challenging questions about whether the selection committee may have had any concerns about appointing him to the role. I asked him to tell me about any times when he had received negative feedback at work. I asked him to give me examples of times when he had been involved in disagreements with colleagues. Though this line of questioning can seem quite negative, if done sensitively and curiously it can support a client to develop a more balanced view of the past and create a more realistic foundation for their future choices. Highlighting negatives can also motivate a client to work towards improving things that are within their control, which is likely to lead to better outcomes in the future.

Support the client to recognise that there is no going back

Clients who are stuck in a melodramatic conflict narrative often think that the solution to all of their problems is for the villain to disappear and for things to be as if the villain had never come onto the scene. Here's a common example of how this plays out in a modern-day workplace. Alan came to me for coaching to manage a conflict with his colleague Kate. Alan had been part of the senior leadership team for a few years. A year earlier, Kate had joined the team. She had responsibility for a different part of the organisation, but there were times when Alan's team and Kate's team had to work together on various projects and share resources. These occasions had been fraught with conflict, largely due to Alan and Kate's very different leadership styles and their sometimes opposing beliefs about what should be prioritised on these projects. Members on each team tended to support their own leader, so the conflict was often played out vicariously between team members, as well as between Kate and Alan as team leaders. The CEO of the organisation eventually stepped in when Kate went on stress leave. Alan was referred to me for coaching. Alan's initial attitude was that the problem was temporarily resolved – Kate was on stress leave and the person acting in her position was, in Alan's opinion, much less problematic to work with. Alan was convinced that Kate would soon resign, and from his perspective the conflict would then be resolved.

If Alan was going to learn and grow from this experience, he needed motivation to put some effort into the coaching. He needed to see that his belief in an ideal outcome (Kate leaving) was not necessarily going to result in everything being perfectly fine again. I asked him to talk about the impact that his conflict with Kate had had on the members of both his own and Kate's team. I also asked him to put himself in the shoes of his CEO and to describe to me what the CEO thought about their conflict and how it had been handled. In answering these questions, Alan began to realise that even if Kate did resign (which was far from a foregone conclusion), this would only guarantee that there would be no future conflict between him and Kate. It did not undo the consequences of their past conflicts. There were still tensions between members of their teams that remained despite Kate's current absence as their leader. The CEO still had concerns about the way Alan had managed the situation, which could have implications for Alan's prospects for future promotion within the organisation. Alan began to recognise that there were things he could do to improve the future – to rebuild relationships between the team members and to impress the CEO with his capacity to repair the damage done. His engagement with coaching dramatically improved and he started to make some very positive changes in his workplace and his leadership style.

Support the client to recognise that they can improve

Clients who come to me for conflict coaching generally want their conflict to be resolved, and I'm more than happy to help them explore ways they might be able to achieve this goal. However, almost always there are opportunities for the client to do more than simply resolve their most immediate conflict situation. They can learn from reflecting on this conflict, so that they can prevent similar kinds of conflicts occurring in the future, or they can develop skills and confidence to manage potential future conflicts early and constructively. When I work with clients in conflict, I try to get them to be future focused, and this means focusing on the future beyond the resolution of this particular conflict.

In a coaching session, when a client comes up with an action plan that they feel is likely to achieve their goal for the coaching session, I never let them continue without asking them a question like, "How can you add value to that plan?" or "What else can you do to make the impact of that plan even better in the long term?" Another useful big-picture question to ask clients is "What can you take from this experience that you can use to improve your future?"

Help the client realise that the future is something they can create

Even when a client believes that they have little control over their own future, when they feel as though their fate has been sealed by the events of the past, we can support them to identify areas in their future where they do have some control. For example, Imogen decided in the course of coaching that the only feasible choice for her to make was to resign from her current role and remove herself from a toxic environment at work (one that she had not been responsible for creating). Though Imogen felt quite disappointed and trapped by her past experience in this workplace, I was able to help her take back some control over her own future. Though these were small steps, they were important for her psychological well-being and resilience. For example, I asked her how she planned to resign. This allowed her to identify a variety of options that were within her control that she could choose between. She came up with options including resigning orally or in writing, giving notice right away or at a later date, offering her employer a short or long notice period, and providing more or less information about reasons for leaving.

Imogen and I then had a conversation about her future job hunting. I asked her what kinds of things she was going to look out for, and ask about, when she was considering a new role. She identified (from her experience in her current role) some of the key warning signs that a workplace might not be a healthy one, and she thought about the kind of research she could carry out to identify those before accepting a position in a new organisation.

Imogen left her current role with some sadness and, honestly, some scars from her very negative experience. However, she also stepped into the future feeling optimistic about her ability to find (and thrive in) a new role that was more aligned to her needs and values.

Conclusion

There is a significant difference between reflecting on and learning from the past and returning to the past. The former emphasises moving forwards, the latter going backwards. In coaching, we want to support clients to keep moving forwards, to learn, grown, and improve from their experiences (good or bad). We are not simply aiming for conflict resolution; we are aiming for our client's transformation.

REFERENCE

Hardy, S. 2008. Mediation and genre. *Negotiation Journal* 24(3): 247–268.

15

SUFFERING TO LEARNING

Both melodrama and tragedy involve suffering. Melodrama approaches suffering as something that should not ever happen and something that is created by evil villains with bad intentions. Tragedy, however, considers suffering as an inevitable part of life. It does not deny that it is unpleasant but suggests that all suffering contributes to learning. In fact, tragedy teaches us that it is through our suffering that we learn the most about ourselves and our place in the world.

When people are suffering (either physically or psychologically) it is a natural human reaction to try to put that suffering out of our minds, to ignore it or try to distract ourselves from it. However, if we do this, we will not learn and grow from the experience and we will suffer for nothing. One of the important roles for the coach to play when working with clients in conflict is to support them to focus on their suffering, to observe it and analyse it, so that they can learn from it. Much of the groundwork for this learning has already occurred in the other shifts (discussed in the previous chapters), but it is important that the coach

DOI: 10.4324/9781003128038-15

specifically ask the client to reflect on their learning from their experiences (both positive and negative) in this conflict. The seeds have already been planted, and the coach helps the client nurture them by giving them specific attention.

When we are working with clients in conflict, the final shift that we want to help them make is to learn from their conflict experience and create some benefit from any suffering that they have experienced. Clients are usually pretty good at talking about their suffering. It is an integral part of the melodramatic conflict narrative – they need to show that the villain has made them suffer (unjustly) to access dream justice. However, clients tend to focus on their suffering as a negative and can find it hard to take any positive from the experience. As a coach, we can help them think about suffering in a different way.

Conflict helps us learn about ourselves, about others, and about the way the world works. Some of the things we may learn when we develop a tragic sensibility about our conflict include that we are not as virtuous as we would like to think (we, too, have flaws), that other people are not (usually) inherently evil, and that life is not always fair. We also learn how to manage our conflicts better, now and in the future. We can also learn how to take responsibility for our own well-being, even in difficult circumstances. We can develop the resilience necessary to continue into the future.

We are not as virtuous as we would like to think

When we deeply reflect on our conflict and we make the shift from a melodramatic conflict story to a more tragic version of events, we often learn that the virtue to which we held tight as the fundamental basis for our claims is slightly tarnished (and sometimes significantly damaged). While it can be uncomfortable to let go of an image of ourselves as entirely virtuous, the shift to vulnerability is essential if we are to learn and grow. To paraphrase Leonard Cohen (1992), the cracks are where the light gets in.

Remember Claire, who was in conflict with her flatmate Alison (Chapter 3)? Claire is a great example of this kind of learning through suffering. As I worked with Claire to reflect on her conflict situation, she learned some important things about herself. She learned that she was not always clear about her expectations of others, even when she felt those expectations very strongly. She also recognised that she often developed resentment towards people who did not meet her expectations, despite the fact that they may not even know about her expectations. Claire knew that she was a conflict avoider, but through this coaching she also realised that she could sometimes be a conflict creator. When she held strong expectations of others but didn't express those clearly to the people concerned, she was inevitably creating conditions for negative conflict. Combine that with subsequent conflict avoidance and you end up with a situation much like the one in which Claire and Alison found themselves: a situation that need never have arisen and that had escalated to a point that was almost ridiculous in hindsight. When I asked Claire what else she had learned during our coaching she paused for a moment, looked sheepish, and then said, "I realise I have behaved like a bit of a bitch towards her."

Claire and Alison's relationship may or may not have been redeemable at this point. It was much more likely to be possible if Claire was able to approach her with an apology for her contributions to the situation and some simple suggestions for getting their flatmate relationship back on track. However, even if it was too late to restore that relationship, Claire learned important lessons that she could take into future accommodation arrangements. She would be much more likely next time she was interviewing potential flatmates to ask specific questions about their expectations about food sharing and to be clearer about what she expected. She may even choose to live alone in future, to have complete control over everything that was in her fridge and pantry!

Other people are not (usually) inherently evil

When Angela first spoke about her conflict with Georgia (Chapter 3), she portrayed Georgia as someone who was inherently evil, who was making Angela suffer because she enjoyed it. By the end of her first coaching session with me Angela had already realised that her own suffering was not necessarily caused by Georgia being deliberately nasty. Instead, she started to recognise that Georgia was likely suffering herself, and Angela came to understand the different contextual factors that were contributing to

Georgia's suffering. These included the fact that Georgia was the oldest and longest-standing staff member, that Georgia was the only employee without a university degree, and that Georgia was perhaps starting to feel irrelevant or underskilled compared to all her newer and more academically educated colleagues. This new understanding helped Angela to develop compassion for Georgia and to recognise that her behaviour was more a response to all of those conditions than to Angela in particular.

Even when life is unfair, we can still choose to learn and grow

Remember George (Chapter 8), who was treated unfairly by the church and who had a legal entitlement to melodramatic dream justice but chose not to take it? George suffered as a result of illegal prejudice. It was unfair and he shouldn't have had to suffer in this way. However, George did not wallow in self-pity or develop a bitter hatred for the people and the church who treated him so badly. Rather, he learnt from the experience and took active steps to improve his situation. He became proactive in searching for similar opportunities in organisations without religious affiliations. He recognised that he had many valuable qualities that could benefit such organisations and that it was a pity that some of those run by churches would not ever avail themselves of what he had to offer. He no longer thought of the church and the people who ran his organisation as perfect; he had witnessed first-hand their flaws. He had suffered at their hands. Yet, he forgave them for their sins. He forgave them and set himself free to find an organisation that accepted him, welcomed him, and valued him for himself.

Exploring our suffering helps us identify our values and act more intentionally

Suffering sometimes draws our attention to our values and can motivate us to choose to live by them in a more intentional way. This is well-illustrated by Polly's family conflict. Polly came to me with about a conflict she had had recently with her teenage sons. She described an interaction in which one of her sons complained that she had not bought enough steak for dinner and how angry she had been about his lack of gratitude. She felt that she may have overreacted at the time, by refusing to have dinner with the rest of her family that night. I asked her to explain to me how she felt at the time her son complained to her. She described feeling angry. I asked her to tell me more about what she was angry about. As Polly talked in more detail about how she was feeling, she shared additional information relevant to what had happened. She mentioned that she was the one who primarily had responsibility for cooking meals for her family, as well as managing the household, and that her sons did not always appreciate how much she did for them. She also talked about how she, herself, was vegan and that if it was up to her she wouldn't be buying meat at all. It had been an unpleasant experience for her just having to touch the packet of meat at the shop. She also explained that one of the reasons she bought that particular packet of meat was that it seemed to have enough in it for all of the boys, and so she only had to touch one pack. Polly also explained that the meat had been quite expensive, particularly because, for her family's health, she insisted on buying the most healthy organic meat without any steroids or other chemicals.

Though in one sense this conversation simply highlighted Polly's suffering and justified it in terms of her values, what it also did was help Polly to learn why the situation had been so triggering for her and why her reaction had been so extreme. It wasn't just about her sons being ungrateful; there were also layers of suffering created because her values (being vegan, eating healthy organic food, looking after her family, and not spending money unnecessarily) had been impacted. Polly began to understand why she had reacted so strongly in that moment, and she also developed the language to be able to explain this to her sons. Finally, she also considered whether, in future, she would be willing to buy and cook meat for her sons or whether it might be better to ask them to do that for themselves. She recognised that part of her emotional response was because she had not put clear boundaries in place around her values and had been resentful of having to purchase the meat in the first place.

Take responsibility for our own well-being

We can also learn how to take responsibility for our own well-being, even in difficult circumstances. We can develop the resilience necessary to continue into the future.

Remember Beverly, who had resigned from her role as president of the board but remained as a general board member and was suffering from her conflict with the new president (Chapter 12)? What Beverly learnt from her coaching was that though the conflict may have been unfair and unnecessary, she didn't have to engage in it. She realised that for her own well-being it was a better choice for her to simply resign from the board altogether rather than expend energy (and expose herself to more suffering) trying to manage and resolve the conflict. It's important to note here that Beverly's decision to resign was not simply a strategy to avoid having to manage the conflict any further. Rather, she made a considered decision about what was in her own (and the association's) best interests at that point in time.

Conclusion

What do we learn about our suffering when we reflect on it with a tragic sensibility? We learn that the world is not always fair. We learn that sometimes good people do bad things. We learn that conflict is more complicated that we recognise at first. We learn that though we may not always be able to get what we want, we always have choices about how to respond to whatever happens. We learn to be better prepared for conflict in the future. We learn to be explicit about our needs and values. We learn to set boundaries. We learn to forgive ourselves and others for our flaws. We learn that new growth can sprout from the ashes.

**USEFUL QUESTIONS TO FACILITATE THE SHIFT
FROM SUFFERING TO LEARNING:**

- What if you were actually planted and not buried? What might be starting to grow?
- In what ways might this be an opportunity in disguise?
- How has this struggle built your confidence for the future?
- What is your future self taking from this experience?
- What limiting beliefs can you leave behind after this experience?
- What and who have you found valuable during this challenge? How are you going to cultivate those things and people in your future?
- What can you contribute to others as a result of this experience?
- Looking back at this experience, what are you grateful for?

- What strengths have you developed during this conflict?
- What has this experience taught you about yourself?
- What can you forgive yourself for? What can you forgive others for?

REFERENCE

Cohen, L. 1992. Anthem [Song]. On *The future*.

16

THE REAL CONFLICT COACHING SYSTEM™

The six shifts discussed in the previous chapters will help someone in conflict to shift from an unhelpful melodramatic version of events towards a more realistic tragic sensibility from which they can learn and grow. However, the shifts do not occur naturally for most people, even if they are well-intentioned about engaging in reflection about their experiences. Having a support person like a coach to facilitate that process makes a significant difference.

Facilitating someone to move through these shifts is more likely to be effective if it is done in a purposeful, rather than ad hoc, way. However, it is also helpful if the person in conflict finds that the conversation feels natural, rather than an overly structured and tedious process. The REAL Conflict Coaching System™ was designed to provide a semistructured but natural process to support a person to reflect on their conflict experiences and develop a more constructive conflict story and future action plan.

The REAL Conflict Coaching System™ provides a useful framework for a coach to support a client through these shifts. The REAL System™ was

DOI: 10.4324/9781003128038-16

developed to provide a practical process for working with clients to support them to develop a more constructive conflict story. It is premised on the basis that the features of a tragic story are more likely to lead to a more constructive response and more conflict resilience. The philosophical underpinnings of the system reflect this. REAL is an acronym that stands for the four pillars of our system: reflection,[1] engagement, artistry, and learning. All four concepts are fundamentally part of stories in the tragic genre. In tragedy, the story revolves around the tragic hero engaging in reflection about how he got into this mess and what his choices might be for getting out of it. In tragedy, the hero engages with the conflict, rather than simply trying to avoid it and waiting for someone to save him. The hero also has the potential to develop artistry – the process of reflection and engagement provides opportunities to do better than the person might think possible. We encourage our clients to work towards improvement and growth, not just a return to the status quo. Finally, tragedy is all about learning – whether the outcome is good or bad, the hero learns and grows in some important way.

The REAL Conflict Coaching System™ aims to support clients to develop what we call the five Cs: clarity, comprehension, choices, competence, and confidence. Clarity refers to the client gaining a level of mindfulness about what has happened and what the situation is for them right now. It is about recognising all of the information that is available to them about their situation, some of which they may have been ignoring or discounting. It is about separating fact from assumption and acknowledging uncertainty. Comprehension refers to the client increasing their understanding of the various factors that have influenced the situation and what is most important to them (and others) now and in the future. Choices refers to the client recognising and reviewing past choices (good and bad) and identifying and evaluating the choices available to them for moving forward. Competence refers to the client increasing their skills in managing the conflict in the future; we also give the client opportunities to practice, reflect, and develop so that they gain confidence to implement their skills and make their future choices after coaching.

The process that we use to achieve these goals is a coaching model that draws from narrative therapy, theories of coaching, and conflict resolution research and practice. The stages in the model are ordered in a particular way to maximise the opportunities for the client to develop a greater clarity and comprehension of their current story and to develop choices for the future (illustrated in Figure 16.1). The stages are also a natural progression for the client during a coaching session, because they are based around the typical storytelling process.

In a normal coaching session (that is, not an intake or exit session) we follow an eight-stage process. The first stage (goal setting) and the last two stages (reflection and closure) are the "bookends" of each coaching session and should always be included. In between those bookends are three stages focused on the past (what happened, why does it matter, and other perspectives) and two stages focused on the future (preferred future and action steps).

Figure 16.1 The REAL Conflict Coaching System™

The eight stages are designed to be followed in order so that they develop the client's thinking in an intentional way. When clients first come to coaching, they tend to think and talk about their conflict in a disorganised and incomplete way. This makes it difficult for them to develop constructive conflict management strategies. The REAL Conflict Coaching System™ stages are designed to help the client order and scaffold their thoughts and develop their thinking in a constructive way. Although, having said that, unless the coach specifically draws attention to the stages and the shifts between them, most clients would not notice the structure or feel that it is restrictive, because each stage flows naturally from the one before.

The stages are designed to build on one another. If the coach jumps forward (for example, straight into action planning without first establishing a clear goal and an in-depth understanding of what happened, why it matters, and other people's perspectives), the action steps are likely to be built on a shaky or incomplete foundation. The more time spent in the earlier stages, the more considered, more effective, and more lasting the client's action plan is likely to be.

However, there are some circumstances in which a coach might be a little bit flexible with the ordering of a coaching session. As we become more skilled at coaching and develop beyond a competent practitioner towards the level of artistry, there are opportunities to be flexible with the order and the way that we use the stages of the REAL Conflict Coaching System™. However, if a coach decides to conduct the stages out of the usual order, this needs to be done intentionally with a very clear purpose and not just because it can sometimes seem easier than managing the stages as they are designed to be used.

As a client moves through the stages, it is frequently the case that something comes up in a later stage that has not been explored in detail in an earlier stage. For example, a client comes up with an action step based on something that has happened in the past and that past incident has not been discussed yet in the session – the coach may do a brief exploration of that past incident before returning to the action steps stage. In this situation, it is perfectly acceptable, time permitting, to go back and do this exploration before moving forward again. Circling back through the process is natural and helpful, but it can be risky to jump forwards without doing the work in the earlier stages.

There are, however, some situations in which a coach might jump from goal setting to preferred future and conduct a solution-focused type of process. Though this is risky in the sense that the client's preferred future and action steps may not be based on as much clarity or comprehension as might be gained from the earlier stages, in some cases this might be the most that is possible. This might happen, for example, where a client needs to have an action plan by the end of one session. They may have an important meeting the following day that they need to prepare for and they simply don't have time to spend going over the past between now and then, or they've got two hours with the coach and they need an action plan by the end of that time. If that's the case, the coach and client cannot spend two hours exploring the past, because this will not leave any time to plan action steps. This is also a good reminder of the importance of clarifying the client's goal at the start of a session, to check whether there is any urgency for the current session, so that the coach can structure the session time most effectively to meet the client's needs.

In most situations, each coaching session should start at the beginning of the system (with goal setting) and then move through the stages in order to the end (reflection and closure). However, in a typical coaching session of 60–90 minutes, there may not be time to do every stage in a lot of detail. Depending on the overall coaching assignment (the number of sessions the client has with the coach) and any urgency in the timing of action planning, the coach may need to spend less time or even skip some of the stages in a coaching session. However, in every session, the coach should always start at goal setting and always leave time (about 10–15 minutes) for reflection and closure at the end. These stages should never be skipped.

What we do in the middle can vary a little bit from session to session. In early sessions, the what happens stage can take up a large percentage of the session. In a first session, the coach and client might work through goal setting, what happened, and a little bit of why does it matter. Then, when there is about 15 minutes left in the session, the coach may skip the rest of the stages and move into reflection and closure.

In a second session, the coach should start at the beginning, rechecking the client's long-term goals and asking the client what their goal is for this particular session. The client and coach may then spend some time in the what happened stage, perhaps adding to the history discussed in the previous session or talking about what has happened since the last coaching session. The what happened stage may be more about reviewing the client's implementation of their action plan from the previous sessions rather than rehashing the long-term history of their conflict situation. In later sessions, if there have not been significant changes to the client's situation over the coaching assignment, there may not be new events to unpack in the what happened stage or a need to go over the past another time. In later coaching sessions the client and coach may move fairly quickly through these early stages and spend more time talking about the future and action planning.

Each stage of the process includes a number of the different shifts, and some shifts will be developed across a number of stages. For example, the goal setting stage promotes a shift of past to future and dependence to agency. The what happened stage includes shifts from simple to complex and certain to uncertain and also lays the foundations of the passive to active shift. The why does it matter stage contributes significantly to the suffering to learning shift, and this shift is also specifically reinforced in the reflection stage. The other perspectives stage helps develop the certain to uncertain shift (particularly in relation to other people's intentions). The preferred future stage is clearly aimed at developing the past to future shift. The action steps stage emphasises the passive to active shift and the dependence to agency shift. Finally, the reflection stage is focused heavily on developing the client's learning from their experience.

Clients who work with me (and other coaches who use the REAL Conflict Coaching System™) report that they experience the coaching process as a fairly natural conversation, in which they are encouraged to slow down and think more deeply about their conflict experience. During coaching sessions they often realise that they knew more than they thought about the situation and that they had more choices than they had recognised coming into the session. Clients frequently say that they leave the session feeling much more empowered to take control of their own future and better understanding themselves and others.

Note

1 For a thorough overview of the use of reflection in conflict resolution practice, see Michael D. Lang's book *The Guide to Reflective Practice in Conflict Resolution* (2019).

REFERENCE

Lang, M. D. 2019. *The guide to reflective practice in conflict resolution.* Lanham, MD: Rowman and Littlefield.

INDEX

Note: *italicised* page references indicate illustrations, **bold** ones indicate tables, and the suffix 'n' indicates a note.

Printed in the United States
by Baker & Taylor Publisher Services